Dear Dana

That Time I Went Crazy
and Wrote All 580 of
My Facebook Friends
a Handwritten Letter

Amy Weinland Daughters

swp

SHE WRITES PRESS

Published 2022
Printed in the United States of America
Print ISBN: 978-1-64742-900-3
E-ISBN: 978-1-64742-406-0

Library of Congress Control Number: 2021921002

For information, address:
She Writes Press
1569 Solano Ave #546
Berkeley, CA 94707

She Writes Press is a division of SparkPoint Studio, LLC.

Book design by Stacey Aaronson

To Dana Dugas Rivera: Thanks for writing me back.

*To Parker Rivera: Can't wait to, at the perfect moment,
meet you in person.*

To Dick and Sue Weinland:
*Thanks for encouraging me to follow through on every single
ridiculous idea I've ever had.*

Prologue

I joined Facebook in August 2008. I had attended a reunion at Camp Olympia in Trinity, Texas, the summer camp I'd grown up at, worked for, and eventually met my husband at.

It was also the font of many of my closest friendships, including Christy Jung McAlister, whom I'd been besties with since 1991. It was Christy who encouraged me to—or, rather, told me I was going to—register for a Facebook account.

I hadn't been at all interested in social media and had never joined any of its early formats, such as MySpace. That's ironic, because I love the idea of reconnecting with people. Reunions had always intrigued me, and, despite my lack of experience with them, they emotionally resonated on a level that made no sense.

I also love shenanigans, and being the center of attention, and being ridiculous. As it turned out, social media and I were a match made in heaven. I just didn't know it yet.

I officially went online on August 27, 2008, adding my first eight friends and writing my first-ever post on Christy's timeline.

> Are you putting Sour Patch Kids and a special helmet from rocketry in your evacuation room? Hoping the hurricane avoids NOLA completely! Thanks for telling me to get on FB —I've gotten nothing done all day and I LOVE IT! Let the toilets clean themselves!

The next day, I updated my status for the first time in history, setting the standard for all the tomfoolery to come.

Amy Weinland Daughters is doing morning aerobics and yoga in a unitard.

It didn't take long for Facebook to become a big part of my everyday life, to the point that now, a decade later, it's difficult to imagine a day where I don't check in on social media at least once (or fifteen, or twenty-five times).

As much as social media has transformed my daily routine, I could never have known that August 27, 2008, the day I joined Facebook, would eventually alter the entire course of my life—relationally, emotionally, and spiritually.

It would take a while, but nothing was ever going to be the same again.

The Road to 1986

Camp Olympia has long been the epicenter of my life. A summer sports camp in the piney woods of East Texas, Olympia was founded by former University of Texas football players and close friends Chris Gilbert and Corby Robertson. In 1968, as underclassmen at UT, the two envisioned a summer program that would be heralded as the best not only in Texas but in all the world.

In the eyes and hearts of many Olympians, including me, the two achieved their goal by creating a place that is like a relational microwave. In the same way that you can zap a frozen pot pie in a microwave in a quarter of the time it would take in a conventional oven, at camp you can acquire a best friend in mere weeks, compared with the years it takes outside the front gates.

In some cases, a three-week camp session is enough to earn you a lifetime friendship. Though the exact chemistry involved is a mystery, it must have something to do with living in close proximity to a dozen kids and being totally removed from your normal life. Temporarily forced into a bubble, you find that the established rules of engagement and even the seemingly concrete boundaries of time are altered, allowing lasting impact to occur more rapidly.

I was introduced to Olympia, and the concept of camping in general, by my BFF in elementary school, Catherine Gilbert.

Her brother, George, attended Olympia with one of his close friends. Eventually, Catherine's parents, Edna and George, convinced mine, Dick and Sue, that Catherine and I should go as well.

It was 1980, a different era in parenting and information technology. Different enough that my parents dropped me, having never seen Olympia's facility or met any of its staff, at a charter bus north of Houston to take the hour-and-a-half journey to Trinity. Along with a fresh bowl cut, I had a new Zebco fishing reel, a metal footlocker, and a stationery set to write letters home.

As with other significant turning points for me, I had no idea that when I stepped on that bus, my life would change forever.

After that first session, I was hooked. I fell in love with the program, the people, and, more than anything, the way the place made me feel. Though I was loved in my regular life, I had a difficult relationship with my mother and struggled with self-esteem issues. At camp, I felt accepted and even celebrated among the green buildings and tall pines. My years after that were defined by going to camp in the summer, missing it in the fall, and anticipating it in the spring. It was, even as I got older, everything.

In the second semester of my junior year of high school, driving and beginning to mature, I applied to be a counselor for the summer of 1985. I'll never forget pulling into the driveway after school and seeing a handmade poster on the back door, complete with balloons, that read, "Amy Weinland—Camp Olympia Counselor." I don't know that my mom had ever made anyone else a poster, but she understood deeply how much the acceptance letter meant to me.

I worked one two-week session that summer and realized

immediately that being a counselor at Camp Olympia was even more fruitful than the experiences I cherished as a camper. I knew I wanted to do it for as long as they would let me.

I turned eighteen in April 1986 and graduated from Klein Oak High School in May. My long-term plans were to attend Texas Tech University in the fall, and my immediate objective was to work the first two terms of the summer at camp.

Looking back thirty years later, I don't know what kind of girl, or young woman, I was going into that summer. Too much of real life separates the fifty-year-old version of me from the eighteen-year-old girl who excitedly packed her trunk that long-ago May. However, from pictures, I can see that 1) I shouldn't have had a perm, 2) I should have had my sister help me with my clothing, and 3) the braces—not good.

And what I can confirm absolutely is that I struggled with self-confidence, was a terrible mouth breather, and was mildly to totally obnoxious. I'm sure of those things because they're all still true.

Summer 1986-November 2013

$\mathcal{S}$ummer 1986 was when I became a permanent fixture on the Olympia staff. Six weeks turned into nine when the camp asked me to stay on for the third session. It was also then that I began to develop long-term relationships that would have incredible staying power. It was the beginning of me finding my people.

I don't remember the actual moment I met Dana Dugas. We shared a cabin, but not for the entire six weeks we were both at Olympia. Living together in a camp setting for even half that time meant we got to know each other very well, very quickly. I do remember a lot of laughter and a few deep conversations.

I can recall sitting outside our cabin one night and telling Dana about my mom, sharing details of the verbal and physical altercations that had occurred between us. After telling her about how, that same year, my mom had locked me out of the house, igniting an ugly incident that included her putting my hand through a window, I said, "Other than my high school best friend, you're the only person I've ever told that to."

I remember Dana reaching over and putting her hand on mine. "That's not right. You've got to tell other people," she insisted. "People who can help you."

As our brief time together rolled on, the sharing continued both ways. I told her about how I was beyond ready to leave home but scared to set out on my own.

"I don't know if I'm ready for college," I said. "I don't know even one person at Texas Tech."

"Listen," she advised, "if you can do this—camp—you can do anything. I've done college, and I absolutely know you can do it and do it well. Leaving home might set you free. That's how you become you."

It was an extraordinary series of conversations, not just then, when I was still living in my parents' home and didn't have proper perspective on what was happening in real time, but now, three decades later. The unwarranted trust that we shared in that brief encounter in 1986 resurfaced and blossomed into something much more powerful in 2015.

After that, I felt a natural kinship with Dana. Not only was it as if we belonged together, cracking ourselves and other people up with our huge personalities, but I felt a kind of peace by being in the same place with her. My crap suddenly felt more together with her in the picture.

I had also met Dana's future husband, Jim Rivera, the previous summer. I had always thought that she had followed him to camp; they both attended LSU and came from Louisiana. They were four years my senior, finishing up in Baton Rouge while I was just getting started in Lubbock.

Jim and Dana got engaged that summer, at a dance club in Huntsville called Shenanigans. It was big news, and perhaps the only midcamp public engagement during our era at Olympia.

The only physical documentation I have of Dana's and my brief meeting in time are a couple of pictures in a small photo album I made of that summer. It was one of those cheap paper albums that come complimentary with photo processing. On the back of the photos, I wrote, "Dana Dugas—Camp Olympia, First Term, 1986."

Even without the photos, which didn't resurface until I had two kids and had moved several times, I would have remembered Dana. Her name had a resilience that is impossible to explain, even in retrospect.

Sadly, Dana and I lost contact when we walked away from the summer of 1986. As far as I knew, she and Jim got married and started a family. As for me, I went off to Texas Tech and continued working at camp during the summers.

I graduated from Tech in 1991. With few job prospects, I agreed to work one final summer at Olympia, as the division head of the intermediate girls. I, along with my parents, felt like it was a bit of a copout—that perhaps I should have been looking for a "real" job, instead of frolicking in the pines one last time.

For all the summer of 1991 wasn't in my search for gainful employment, it was epic—in a once-in-a-lifetime way—relationally. It was the summer I met my future husband, Willie, who was similarly avoiding "real" life after graduating from West Texas State. Willie and I met at the front gates of camp, where I was tasked with greeting arriving first-year staff with misinformation and half-truths. From there, we were placed in a fishing class together—I as the teacher and he as the assistant—by a friend who saw us as a viable situation.

"Now, boys," I told the small group of campers we led to the fishing site, "I'll be your teacher, and this fine, strapping young man is my assistant."

I sounded like Barney Fife, but for me, I guess that was putting out the vibe.

About two weeks into the class, Willie asked me what I liked to eat. "Maybe we could go grab a bite?" he said, not knowing that he was going to be having dinner with me for the rest of his life.

Two nights later, we were at the local El Chico, eating nachos. By midsummer, we were a budding camp romance. By August, he had returned home and I was helping close up camp for the summer. Standing at the pay phone by the maintenance shed on a humid East Texas night, he told me he loved me for the first time.

"I love you too," I replied, and hung up. Dumbfounded, I immediately deposited seventy-five additional cents, called him back, and asked, "Did you really just say that?"

"Yep!" he replied.

Twenty-two months later, my dad was walking me down the aisle.

It's been said that Willie is the male version of me. If there is any truth to that, he's like Amy 3.0—a much-improved version with upgraded intelligence, positivity, and kindness.

That was also the summer I hooked up with a wide swath of people who would become my lifelong BFFs, including Patty Buchanan Lanning, Dawn Oldham Koenig, and Christy Jung McAlister—the same special someone who would force me to join Facebook seventeen years later.

Willie and I married in 1993 and settled in Houston, both with real jobs. We welcomed our first son, Will, in 1997. In 2002, Willie's employer gave us the opportunity to move overseas to England, where a two-year plan was extended to three. We returned to Texas in 2005 and welcomed our second son, Matthew, in February 2006. Soon after, we got the call to move to Dayton, Ohio, where we would live for twelve years.

Though Dana and I had zero contact during those years, I couldn't ever get her name out of my mind. Occasionally, I would stop and wonder, *What ever happened to Dana?* But I suppose that wasn't unusual, as camp relationships had resonated with me for years.

I remained in close contact with Olympia even before Willie and I sent Will, and then Matthew, there as campers. I was a founding member of the fledgling alumni association. One night in the late 1990s, I was in the camp office with a group of alumni tasked with making calls asking people to attend the biannual reunion in Trinity.

From my phone station, I asked, "Whatever happened to Jim and Dana Rivera?"

"They have a bunch of kids and live in Louisiana," someone answered, handing me a computer printout. "Here's their number. Call them."

I dialed the number, and nobody picked up, but they had an answering machine. I left a message, which, as far as I know, no one ever replied to. It was the only direct contact I would have with the Riveras between 1986 and 2013.

Joining Facebook in 2008 reconnected me with the bulk of my Olympia friends, many of whom I hadn't seen in twenty-plus years. It was exciting to be in touch with so many of the people who had made those summers the best of my life.

Dana's name continued to pop in and out of my mind. I never wondered why I was thinking of her; it was just a part of my subconscious that I never questioned. I even remember looking up her name early in my Facebook days, to no avail.

By 2013, after five years on social media, I had reconnected with most of my past. The act of being in relationship required nothing more than extending or accepting friend requests, so it was easy to try to hook up with as many individuals as had names that I could remember.

In November 2013, Dana's name appeared on my radar again, this time while I was online on Facebook. Typing in her name—Dana Dugas Rivera—I was surprised and delighted to finally find her. Excitedly, and without any forethought, I sent her a friend request.

Dana accepted, and I did what I always did when I got a new "friend," especially one I had been wondering about for years: I clicked on her profile and spent an enjoyable few moments looking through her life.

I liked to begin my stalking by looking at the person's photos. The first thing that struck me was Dana's hair. When we had been at Olympia together, she had had dark, curly hair. Now, twenty-seven years later, it was blond and straight. Somehow, this was a big deal to me. Perhaps that was because I hadn't found keratin yet.

Next, I confirmed that she and Jim did live in Louisiana and did have a bunch of kids—five, to be exact: a bunch of girls and one son. The other fact that resonated with me immediately was that Dana and I had zero mutual friends. This was highly unusual in the world of camp relationships.

I can remember feeling very satisfied by not only finding Dana but reconnecting with her. Accepting my friendship meant, presumably, that she remembered me as well. It was like a major box ticked on a mental checklist that I didn't even know existed. But back then, I thought that was as far as it would go. There is no way I could have imagined the destination we were speeding toward.

Parker

$\mathcal{I}$t didn't take long for me to figure out that Jim and Dana's only son, Parker, had cancer. It was the abiding theme of not only her posts but those of her friends and family, who offered up their support on her timeline (which back then was called a wall).

Parker was being treated at St. Jude in Memphis, which meant he was likely fighting for his life.

The Riveras clearly had lots of support, as Dana's page featured numerous pictures of people wearing "Team Parker" shirts. Everything was LSU themed—purple and gold.

As a fellow mom, I felt Dana's situation resonating immediately with me. It was the worst-case scenario—a precious child with a horrible diagnosis. She was living everyone else's darkest fears.

On one level, I didn't think it was my place to "like" or "comment" on anything I saw in that initial review, nor on the blips about Dana and Parker that began to be a part of my news feed now that we were Facebook official. I was an old memory, living in the shadows of her one summer at Olympia, twenty-seven years earlier. If I couldn't conjure up more than a handful of lucid memories of her from that time, how much of me could she remember?

Then, the day after Christmas—December 26, 2013—Dana

posted a request for prayers, as Parker was staring down a heavy round of treatment:

> We are all good but asking for specific prayer for Parker. We have a HEAVY chemo dose to go through the next few days, and Parker is sensitive to chemo as it is! Asking for minimal suffering through this round! As ALWAYS, thank you for your love, support, and prayers.

This was the moment when I unknowingly, officially crossed over from being an innocent bystander to being an active, though distant and totally undetectable, participant.

Prayer had always been something that I felt drawn to. If I had a spiritual gift—something that was fashionable to discuss at the time—prayer was a strong possibility. It appealed to my deep emotional nature, an undercurrent that I usually kept guarded under layers of silliness. It was private, something no one else could see or comment on.

That also meant that nobody could tell me I was doing it wrong. And since I felt less than confident about how to pull off being a Christian in public, it was something I could do on my own terms. Just me and God.

Additionally, I had always found it easy to focus and find God in those quiet moments removed from the pace of regular life. It wasn't so much that I knew what to say; it was that I could connect with and feel His presence. And I loved the idea of lifting people up without their even knowing it.

Prayer appealed to me on so many different levels. It, like social media, seemed tailor-made for my personality.

I felt personally called by Dana's post. Instead of her requesting prayers from her one thousand–plus Facebook friends, I felt like she was asking me individually to pray.

Instead of commenting on her post, I was compelled to

reach out to Dana directly. The only means of doing this was via a Facebook message, as we obviously didn't have each other's contact information. So I sent her a message, a move that, at that time in my life, was completely out of character for me, because 1) I'm terrible about reaching out to people and do better just being supportive silently—only to later desperately wish I had said something, 2) I had always been way better at thinking of great things to do than at actively following through, and 3) in this specific scenario, the normal me would have understood that whatever relationship I had had with Dana was so far gone that direct contact was a bit bold. And while I could be bold while ribbon dancing in a blue polyester suit, I wasn't that way emotionally.

The fact that I even sent that first message to Dana illustrates how invested I felt in her story only a month into having reconnected with her. Just like when her name had popped into my head repeatedly, for no apparent reason, I didn't question it —I just moved forward, almost as if on instinct.

December 27, 2013

Hi! Just wanted to let you know that we are praying for you and your family today! We will keep praying, and then we will pray some more.

Lots of love,
Amy Weinland Daughters and Family

PS: I'm just as attractive as you may remember I was; if not, I've gotten even better-looking. . . .

PPS: WE ARE PRAYING FOR YOU!!!!!!!!!!!!!!!

The message is a perfect illustration of who I am. I sincerely care about people but feel obliged to throw in some ridiculous bit: *Just in case I've offended or overstepped the mark, here's some-*

thing silly to divert your attention. It's at the intersection of Low Self-Esteem Street and Obnoxious Avenue.

I prayed for Parker and Dana often in the hours and days following my message. I also began checking her Facebook page for updates. Without my even knowing it, my heart was being surrounded by the Riveras.

What I didn't really expect was a reply from Dana. Despite this, she sent me just that a couple of days later.

December 30, 2013

You are too sweet and still so fun!! Thank you so very much for the prayers!!! It really means a lot!!!

The fact that Dana responded to my initial message was even more extraordinary than my reaching out in the first place. She took the time to reply to a random message from a random person, with actual words, while her son was suffering through a chemotherapy treatment. Who even does that? It's very possible that had she not responded to that initial communication, the extraordinary sequence of events that followed would never have happened. It is a testament to how small things we do in "normal," everyday life, without even thinking about them, can morph over time into big things.

Looking back from what was then the future, I know now that Dana was showing her hand. Her personality compelled her to be someone who responded dutifully. Though I would get a lot of credit for reaching out to her as time went on, her commitment to replying, despite her family's dire circumstances, was the real reason our unbelievable connection flourished.

We would repeat this cycle—in which I reached out crazily and she eventually responded—over and over again in the years ahead.

January–November 2014

I continued to pray for and check in on Dana and Parker as the new year arrived. We moved to a new house in the same area of Ohio on January 3. I remember sitting in our new master bathroom, on the carpeted step up to the tub, on move-in day and checking Facebook, then praying hard-core for both of them.

Later in January, I saw posts about Dana and Parker returning home from Memphis. In February, she requested prayers—which I acted on—as Parker suffered through a rough stretch lasting several days. Though they were back in Louisiana, they were still visiting Memphis monthly and also going to weekly treatments in Baton Rouge.

In April, I saw a picture of Parker returning to the eighth grade. Dana was obviously thrilled, and I felt a wash of thankfulness that, even then, seemed a bit much, given our obvious distance in years and miles. It reminded me to pray for the Riveras again, and this time to offer up thanks, along with prayers, for his ongoing treatment.

Though I didn't actively check in on Dana, as I had at the beginning of the year, her posts were a part of my news feed and kept me somewhat informed of how Parker was doing.

As had been the case before, Dana moved back into another part of my consciousness, only this time, our virtual connection on social media made her name come up even more often than it had before. Her signal now blipped even more clearly on my radar.

The mystery of how Facebook decides what we see and don't see has always intrigued me. In this case, I believe that God was manipulating the algorithms, ensuring I was seeing what I was supposed to.

More seeds were being planted.

The summer of 2014 came and went. Matthew attended his first-ever session at Olympia, while Will completed his ninth. The day before we sent our boys off to third and eleventh grades, respectively, in August, I came across a post from Dana that would stay with me for numerous reasons. It was a photo of Parker and Peyton, Jim and Dana's youngest daughter, on the first day of school.

> Time flies!! Parker is LHS freshman #5 for the RIVERAS!!! Love, love, LOVE LHS!! Real-world, A school, prepared for college. Happy first day!

Parker was starting the school year, just like everyone else! I rejoiced in a way that, again, made no sense. Though I felt like the post and photo were a direct answer to my prayers, I hadn't contacted Dana again since my message the previous December.

I see now that God was preparing my heart to be taken over by the Rivera family. Every post meant more than the last.

This was also the moment when my regular prayers dissipated. Even though I had zero evidence of the crisis passing,

Parker's return to school made me assume that Dana and her family were okay. It was also a time in my life where deep prayer was not a regular occurrence. I did talk to God just before bed every night, and I prayed with Matthew. I was also a small-group leader for Will's student ministry program at church, so we obviously prayed there. But as far as earnestly being in dialogue with God daily went, with time set aside exclusively for that purpose, it wasn't happening.

In retrospect, I can see that God and I weren't actively BFFs at the time. While I certainly believed, perhaps my faith wasn't anchored firmly enough to dictate regular time to communicate. It was a very casual connection. Though I was fully aware of His realness, we weren't doing life together.

As the fall progressed, I continued to see Dana on Facebook. I was still excited to be connected to her, enjoying the window into her world that social media provided. A bonus was that she posted often about LSU football. As a passionate lover of college football and someone who had found a way to get paid for writing about it, I appreciated her obvious enthusiasm.

From time to time, she also posted about Parker. He was still receiving treatment, but it all seemed to be happening locally. Additionally, Dana's posts were so positive, I assumed all was well and moved on—still caring, still wondering, but not alarmed.

December 1–14, 2014

*O*n early December, I noticed a brief post from Dana, asking for prayers. It wasn't specific, but I was worried. What did it mean?

I started to pray regularly for the Riveras again. Dana and Parker came to mind continuously, and I just kept thinking, *God, please take care of these people.* Again, I didn't really stop to consider that something unusual was happening. I had lots of friends on Facebook and in real life, and, frankly, while I did remember when I saw a prayer request, it was easy to forget to follow through on it after a day or two.

This wasn't the case with Dana. Her requests felt urgent, as if responding to them silently was the most critical thing I could do in a day. It was a driving force that didn't subside, as it normally would have. It's important to note that I wasn't deliberately putting the Riveras at the top of some sort of priority list; they were just there magically. My brain didn't even stop to consider it; my heart just knew what to do.

The prayers fed my concern. I began checking her profile regularly again and saw that they were heading back to Memphis. That was December 10.

On December 12, a Friday, she asked for more prayers, stating, *We have a lot to get through today!!!* I prayed throughout that day, checking back in with her page for updates.

We arrived in Memphis for a one-night stay, a quick appointment that WE requested, and an X-ray. As we drove up Wednesday night, I thought, "Home Sweet Memphis" and then thought, "Why did I just think that?" Well, God certainly knew why! We found out yesterday that Parker has relapsed. We have had difficulty, as you might guess, with this news and have had a very long day, full of tests, scans, and blood draws. The news we received today was positive; however, the plan is to stay here for the next ten to twelve months. It will be rough, and we will certainly need prayer for the things we will endure, but rest assured we are where we need to be!!! We are surrounded by Love from people who have been with us since day one! And the RMH welcomed us back with open arms, though they were just at capacity! We are very grateful to be where we are—Home Sweet Memphis!! Thanks for your prayers, texts, and love! Health and peace.

Inasmuch as my first message to Dana illustrated who I am, her post spoke volumes about who she is.

First, she shared the news. She took the time to let everyone else know what was going on. Then her tone was positive, even though she couldn't possibly have had any more horrific news to share. Finally, she recognized publicly people who showed her and her family any level of kindness. She was grateful in the face of terror. She was a positive, appreciative sharer. All this even though her dreams were being smashed.

Though this clearly had nothing to do with me, this was the moment when my heart began to go over the edge. While it's logical to assume that anyone, connected or not, would have been gutted by her post, I could physically feel a lump in my throat.

I thought about Dana and Parker as I prayed on and off throughout the next day, a Saturday. On Sunday morning, I went to church. Through much of the service, I found myself praying specifically for the Riveras. I wanted to do something. I needed to do something. I had to do something.

During the closing song, an idea popped into my head. I would write to Dana and Parker in Memphis—Home Sweet Memphis. As soon as I had the notion, I knew I wasn't just going to think about doing it—I was actually going to make it happen.

When we got home, Willie and I were changing in our bathroom. I had shared Dana's posts with him, so he was already familiar with the story. "I'm going to write them in Memphis," I said.

"That's a good idea." he replied, not realizing that he had just agreed to keep the US Postal Service in business.

The next morning, I got up, still fully invested in my new idea. I work from home as a freelance writer, so, after the kids had gone to school, I sat down at my desk and started thinking about logistics. It was then that I realized I had no idea *where* to write Dana.

Though her most recent post had mentioned the Ronald McDonald House, I didn't know if she could receive mail there, or if that was where she would be staying full-time. I decided to have another look at her Facebook page.

Dana had written a long post later in the day Sunday or that night, and I hadn't seen it until just now. It was a twelve-point treatise on all the things she was thankful for, despite Parker's relapse. She was grateful for the doctors, advocates, nurses, and staff; for her friends and neighbors back home; for the people at the RMH; and for fellow parents—now sacred friends—who would battle alongside her.

Her post itself illustrated her extraordinary Dana effect. But for me, the most mind-blowing detail came at the end, after her numbered list. Not only did she confirm that they were indeed staying at the Ronald McDonald House, she included the *full address*.

> Please continue to cover us with prayer, but, as you can see, God has provided LOVE and comfort from many people!! Thank you for your texts, comments, and prayers! I'm putting our address because we've been asked by many and we love to get notes or cards.
>
> Happy Sunday, my friends!!

Boom.

She had given me her address without even knowing it.

Without my even asking.

Could my desire to write Dana and Parker be part of something bigger?

December 15, 2014–January 4, 2015

I initially decided to send Dana and Parker cards because doing so seemed more manageable than writing letters. First, a card had less space to fill—a key element when you're writing somebody whom you don't really know. Next, at the time, it looked less stalker-ish, I supposed—that is, if I was going to keep things real but not too real. Finally, it was the holiday season and I had lots of extra Christmas cards available. I wrote the first card that very morning.

I don't know how many cards I mailed the Riveras from December 15 until the new year arrived. I'm guessing it was at least one per week, plus our family Christmas card, which I remember sending in addition.

While I was visiting Willie's brother and family in College Station, Texas, my sister-in-law, Shelly, drove me around, looking for a mailbox to deposit one of the cards in. Even though I couldn't have known it at the time, this scene—a wild goose chase for a blue box—would become a very common practice in my and my family's lives.

I envisioned writing Dana and Parker until he was released, once again, to Louisiana and his normally scheduled life. On top of this, I was already thinking big. My personality dictated that I went over the top in almost everything, especially when my heart was involved, which meant this wasn't going to be an exception. It didn't seem to matter to me—at all—that I hadn't spoken to or seen Dana in twenty-eight years and had never met Parker.

I had plans to send Dana gift cards from places near the RMH. Google would be helpful, but I guessed Starbucks would be a good start. I would tell her it was my way of taking her out to coffee, if only virtually.

I drove through Memphis at least four times a year, twice on each of our annual road trips to and from Texas. This meant if Dana and I connected through the letters, I guessed I could stop in and say hi at some distant point in the future.

Though this was all pure craziness, it was how I was already thinking during those first few weeks. On the one hand, I realize I come across as a stalker; on the other, and probably closer to the truth, it illustrates how invested I was from the very first word I wrote to Dana. It would take me a long time to figure out even partially what that meant.

I also prayed for the Riveras more and more often. This was as easy as writing the letters; it didn't seem awkward, because it was a part of me. I thought of them frequently enough that praying just seemed like a natural consequence of their being at the forefront of not only my mind but my heart. I never questioned any of this, I just went with it.

As 2014 ended and 2015 began, I noticed that the tone of Dana's posts began to shift. Eventually, it wasn't Dana posting; instead, it was her friends and family, either requesting prayers for the Riveras or directing prayers and love at them.

Though I couldn't be sure, I assumed Parker wasn't doing well.

We went to church on Sunday, January 4. During the service—the first we had attended since December 14, when I was overcome with the idea to write the letters in the first place—I felt an overwhelming sense of urgency to pray for Dana, which I did through much of the hour. Though part of this impulse was clearly due to what I had seen on Facebook, my one and only link to the Riveras, the strong emotional pull I felt went beyond what I would have felt for a similar long-lost friend in crisis.

I hadn't taken my phone with me to church that morning—something that seems almost unthinkable now. I didn't check Facebook until I got home. As I stood in my bathroom, half dressed, the very first item in my news feed was a post from Dana.

> Our precious Parker went to be with Jesus this morning. Our family surrounded him, sang to him, kissed and loved on him, and told him how much we loved him and that it was okay. It is hard to fathom now, but we are so happy he is no longer suffering. The posts you never saw are that he has been through great suffering through this journey, and it had started again! He is no longer in pain, and we are grateful. We had a beautiful day all day yesterday with him, and all of his sisters were here, as well as our son-in-law and grandbaby. Our doctors were also with us all weekend and today. Dr. Inaba was with us from eight thirty Friday morning and finally went home at six last night, only to be back this morning at five. He was with Parker when we left the hospital. Our ICU doctor worked nonstop all weekend, and no test, scan, or transfusion was left on the table. We are grateful. Parker was days from dying when we arrived eighteen months ago, and we are so grateful to have had that time with him. We have spent more time together in the last eighteen months than some people do in twenty years. We will celebrate Parker's spirit for the rest of our lives. He had a walk with Jesus that was beautiful, and he never lost his faith! He accepted every

challenge with a crooked little smile on his face, never complained, and would apologize for throwing up or being sick. He loved family and God so very much! It is fitting that he would go home to be with Jesus on a Sunday!! We cannot thank you enough for the outpouring of love that we have received. We are blessed!! Health and peace, my friends!

I've never been a crier. It's not that I don't want to cry; the tears just have a way of not coming out. This was different. First I sobbed and sat down by the tub. Then I went out and told Willie and Will, still crying. Not used to seeing me in tears, they both hugged me. We exchanged very few words. I felt like Dana and I had spent the past thirty years doing life together. It made no sense, but I couldn't stop crying.

January 5-12, 2015

The only thing I could think of when I considered what to do next was to send a condolence card. Monday morning, January 5, I went to Kroger for groceries and wandered into the greeting-card section. When I got home, I sat down to fill out the card I'd bought. I'm not sure why I didn't think about it sooner, but I immediately realized that I had no clue where I was going to mail it. It wasn't like I could message Dana and say, "Hey, what's your home address?" while she was suffering something I couldn't even imagine. In fact, I wasn't even sure precisely *where* she lived. Was it Lafayette, Baton Rouge, or some other town in that general vicinity?

Though I could never have understood the lasting impact these thoughts would ultimately have, that moment was destined to be another huge turning point. Stepping off the bus at camp. Joining Facebook. Friending Dana. Not having her home address.

My life course was being remapped without my even knowing it.

I had remembered, from Facebook or perhaps through a camp friend, that Jim was a lawyer. I Googled his name and found his law firm in Lafayette. I filled out the address and again used a stamp left over from my Christmas cards.

What I wrote was brief. Though it was the kind of thing you'd say in a sympathy card, the wording was stronger than what you might expect in a message to friends from thirty years ago. I told Jim and Dana that my "heart broke" for them and that I was "devastated on [their] behalf." I also promised to pray for them.

I mailed the card immediately. Dana had to know how I felt, even if she didn't know me.

The rest of that week, I found myself thinking of Dana over and over again. I did pray, a lot, but more than anything, I felt a personal sadness that didn't fit the circumstances. Yes, it was for Dana, but I could feel it emotionally—like something had happened to *my* heart. It was as if the line between sympathy (my feeling genuinely sorry for her) and an actual personal experience was blurring.

The following Sunday, January 11, we were back in church. I spent the entire service asking God what I was supposed to do next with the Riveras. My plan to write Dana and Parker until he was healed was clearly out the window. I had felt so called to that arrangement that I was now at a loss.

Toward the end of the service, again during one of the worship songs, I received a crystal-clear message in the form of an enormous feeling: *Keep writing the letters.* I felt as if I had been commissioned—without anyone else in the world knowing (including Dana).

That next day, I upped my game by visiting Target—which I now know has a better card selection than the folks down at Kroger. There, I purchased several sympathy and "thinking of you" cards.

Back at home, I wrote the very first card that I would address solely to Dana.

January 13–March 16, 2015

I wrote Dana every single week. At the beginning, I didn't have a designated day for her letter; usually, I just found a few quiet moments during my workweek and penned a card. My remarks were brief, extremely so in comparison with the treatises I would write in the future.

I remember clearly having no idea what to say. I knew very little about grief, so I felt strongly that I shouldn't try to offer up any wise (or, in my case, probably unwise) words on what to feel or not to feel. Instead, I wrote about my life and my family, slowly introducing her to my world.

This approach was a direct result of my relationship with a neighbor family in Dayton. Sue Shibley and her kids, Lee and Emma, moved in across the street from us just weeks after we relocated to Ohio from Texas. It was also just months after Sue's husband—a colonel in the US Air Force—had died suddenly, during the family's latest assignment, in Wichita, Kansas.

Sue was open with her feelings, willing to explore everyone's emotional state. She talked freely about the experience of losing her husband so suddenly. She even shared a video that she, Lee, and Emma had made at the grief group they attended.

Though countless little details made an impression on me, two resonated enough to stick. They also carried over, not by accident, into my budding relationship with the Rivera family.

First, Sue taught me that it was okay that I didn't have anything to say about Dana's grief. She also advised me that it was better just to be honest and say, "That totally sucks," rather than trying to rely on clichés about some sort of meaningful journey through losing a loved one.

Next was something that both Sue and her kids mentioned. In the video, Lee and Emma talked about how, right after their dad passed, there were literally hundreds of people on hand, along with cards, food, flowers, and lots of activity.

Then, suddenly, at some undesignated hour, it all stopped. In Lee's words, "the casseroles just stopped coming."

This laid the foundation for my approach to my letter-writing campaign to Dana. First, I didn't have any good words about grief—so, for the most part, I never tried to use any. I just focused on relaying the message of my caring and my nonstop praying. Sue's advice made me feel like this was a viable approach.

Next, though I knew—and still know, and will always know —that I couldn't/can't really do anything for Dana, I could *not* move on. I could keep the casseroles coming.

Sometime during the first few months of writing Dana, I began mentioning "constant" prayer. Eventually, I expressed the concept in hashtag form—as #CONSTANT. I would have done this because my best friend from England, Julia, and I were happily hashtagging wildly in our texts, even though I'm pretty sure we didn't really understand what hashtags were or how they were supposed to be used.

#CONSTANT—which was meant to be a reminder that I was praying for Dana and her family all the time, and that cumulatively, the many people praying for her equaled ongoing, limitless prayers—would become the buzzword in our in-writing relationship. I had no idea how big it would get.

It also kicked off what would be a barrage of hashtags between Dana and me. Some would be hilarious, while others would be part of our most meaningful discourse.

I sent Dana ten cards between January 12 and March 15, all to Jim's law office in Lafayette. On March 16, 2015, a Monday night, I received a Facebook message from her.

March 16, 2015

Sweet Amy!!! Every single card and letter has blessed me more than you will ever know!!! I just am so humbled you would go to such trouble for me!! It is such an outpouring of love!! We are okay—day by day we manage to go through living without our precious Parker! I still can't believe it most days!! We are sooooo lonely for him!!! We are all trying to play the hand we've been dealt as he did—with dignity, grace, and faith—but I have learned he was a much better person than I am! Our girls surround us with love each day, and we have been kept busy by them and activities they've got us doing. We are also BLESSED with wonderful, loving friends who surround us every single weekend and many days during the week. I returned to work, and that helps to keep my mind busy for part of the day. I teach at a school that is very much like a family to me, and they watched Parker grow up as he went to elementary school there, so it is a comfort to be there surrounded by people who love me and my family. And my sweet students are a gift as well!! Jim is leading our family with strength, faith, and love and tries to be so strong for us! Thank you, Amy!!! I look forward to the next note. Here's my home address. Love you, friend!!!

Even now, several years later, I still can't express what this message means to me. To say I was humbled to receive it would be a massive understatement.

My friends and I also refer to it as the "cease and desist" message, only because Dana provided her home address, saving the staff at Jim's office from forwarding another letter on to his house.

March 17, 2015

Hi! I can't begin to tell you what your message means to me. Receiving it has definitely made my week! I am in awe of your strength and honesty, Dana. If my little notes have provided even the slightest level of comfort, then I am the one who is truly blessed. Thanks also for your address; I know the people at Jim's office will be relieved. If they do miss the letters, let me know and I'll drop them a line. I'll keep writing, praying, and hoping for peace for you and your family. Know that you are a blessing to so many people, including me. Love to you, my friend, and THANKS again. #CONSTANT

And so the letters, the praying, and the craziness continued.

March 17–April 25, 2015

$\mathcal{M}$y family went to California for spring break the first week of April. Given that it had been only four months since I had started writing to Dana, it was noteworthy that I found myself looking for cards I could send her during each of the stops we made on our trip.

Back home, I had a very intense series of thoughts after praying for Dana in front of the chair in the corner of my office. While I assumed that the prayers had to be a good thing, what was the letter writing all about? Why was I doing it? What did it mean? Was I putting myself out there unnecessarily, and for no one's real benefit? And was I supposed to keep writing? Those questions wouldn't be answered until much later, and never completely. However, later that evening, I received another crystal-clear message in the form of an overwhelming feeling of pure adrenaline, as if I had just bungee-jumped off a cliff. As with the prayers and my initial plan to write to Dana and Parker in Memphis, I had an absolute sense of what to do. Amid all the things I wasn't sure of in my life, I was sure of this.

I was going to just keep writing the letters.

I turned forty-seven on April 25, which was a Saturday. As is the case with many adult birthdays, not much was going on that day. Willie and Matthew were at a Cub Scouts campout, and Will was doing his second performance of *West Side Story* at the high school.

Our mail was never delivered until late, usually after 6:00 p.m. I didn't check it regularly, because nothing ever happened via mail. That day was different, because it was my birthday and I was home alone. Maybe somebody would surprise me with a card, even though that kind of thing was very rare in 2015.

We lived on a busy road then, and had to get our mail using a door on the back of the mailbox. Reaching in, I pulled out a small stack of envelopes and turned back toward my house. Flipping through them, I got just under our huge tulip magnolia tree and stopped.

There it was: a white envelope addressed, in perfect handwriting that I didn't recognize, to Amy W. Daughters. The return address was inscribed with one of those fancy stamps you can get on Etsy—a big "R" with a circle around it, above the name and address.

It was from Jim and Dana Rivera.

Dana had written me back.

Holy crap.

No matter how much time passes, I will never think it's dramatic to refer to this as one of the greatest moments of my entire life.

I didn't open the letter right away. Instead, I took it inside and held it like it was the Jewel of the Nile. Since I hadn't shared the fact that I was writing Dana with anyone other than Willie and Will, I didn't have anyone to text crazily, *OMG—she freaking wrote me back.*

I finally opened the envelope and found the following message in her impeccable handwriting:

Sweet Amy:

I write this to you from my classroom—hence the fish paper. Much better than loose-leaf, huh?

I must tell you that your cards and letters bring so much joy to my family and me. Your writing talents keep us engaged till the last word. It is hard for me to believe that someone I haven't seen in over twenty-five years would care so much. We have been surrounded by love, but there are many in our inner circle who have moved on (which I understand, because before this, that was me), yet you still make the effort! Wow! "Thank you" seems so inadequate.

We are okay—surviving. I'm quite sure we have reached the "angry" stage, certainly the questioning stage. We are so lonesome for Parker—his physical presence, a hug, a kiss . . . There are moments of joy—our granddaughter (also Amy ☺) took her first steps yesterday ☺—and during the great joy, we are consumed with sadness. Parker "adored" Amy, and he would be so excited she's walking. I am so grateful he got to meet her. He told me a few months back, "I can't imagine loving my own kids more than I love Amy." I am so happy he got to experience that sort of parental love. He spent a lot of time with her, because anytime Jim and I did anything without him, he stayed at Alli's house.

We are trying to live normally. We do things we don't necessarily want to do. I just returned from the beach with Peyton and Mady. We do things for and with our girls. Being together brings us all comfort. The girls have provided great relief for us, as they all "tend" to us, though they are struggling as well. I am so proud of them.

Jim went back to work a week after (the breadwinner ☺), and I came back to work in early March. I teach English Language Arts (regardless of the errors in this letter) to fourth graders. Reading is my main subject, but I also teach writing and a little English. (These days, the curriculum expects kids to learn grammar through telepathy, as it is not a focus ☺.) I have two classes of twenty-three kids, and they are precious. They knew Parker, as he rode the bus here in the afternoons, so they are very sweet and sensitive to my struggles right now. Being at school helps very much—as much as anything can help these days.

Well, my intention was to thank you so very much for your #constant ☺! I didn't mean to ramble, but writing this has actually felt nice, so perhaps I will take a page out of your book and continue. Just know that your kindness, prayers, and love are appreciated.

Health, peace, and love, my friend!!

Dana

PS: I hope this was not too much of a "downer." It is not my intention to depress anyone. I just started writing, and this is what came out ☺.

The letter, like her approach on Facebook, spoke so much about who Dana is. First, she shared openly. Next—and this is perhaps the thing I admire most about her—she was honest, not only about her situation but about herself (i.e., "that was me").

Finally, she was grateful and super-positive, to the point that she didn't want to be a "downer" or "depress anyone," even though she was going through hell.

For me, her commentary on people "moving on" especially resonated, and does even more so now, as I look back on our story after the passage of several years. Her observations are the same as those of the Shibley kids, Lee and Emma, who, magically, were also part of my reasoning for continuing to write to Dana. Like so many layers of the story of Dana and me, it was no coincidence.

Finally, Dana's words about how writing the letter made her feel—both that it "felt nice" and "I just started writing, and this is what came out"—foreshadowed the transformative impact of all the letters we had not yet written.

Though receiving a letter is a wonderful emotional experience, writing one provides a therapeutic release that is difficult to describe in words.

April 26–June, 2015

*D*ana's first letter was a milestone in our connection: It was the moment we became pen pals. It also encouraged me, in a characteristically off-the-charts way, to keep writing. Finally, Dana's reply ramped up my efforts to pray for her and her family even more.

I had also began using the Jesus Calling devotional app for my iPhone. It provides a daily message that's presented in the first person, as if God—whose "dialogue" is based on included biblical references—is addressing the reader personally. Either it enhanced my praying or it was the other way around, and the praying compelled me to do the devotionals.

I wasn't listening to God as much as He was relentlessly pursuing me via the Riveras. It would be a mistake to imagine me standing in a field of golden wheat in a white dress, trying to hear what God was saying—asking Him what He wanted me to do. Instead, it was more like I was doing my own thing, not in a field, in yoga pants, and He took over my heart and made me think it was all my idea.

It all added up to my *wanting* to do it—the praying, the letters, the drawing closer to God—as opposed to feeling like I had to. Again, and with feeling, God knew who He was dealing with.

My family and I left for Texas on May 27 to take Will and Matthew to Camp Olympia. It was the first time Willie and I had both boys at camp at the same time; we were kidless for two full weeks.

I continued to write to and pray for Dana. Carrying stamps and cards with me at all times became a regular part of life, as did looking for post offices and blue mailboxes. I began to share more and more with Dana, compelled to fill the blank spaces in the cards with entertaining information and details of my not-so-interesting life. I realized I had lots to say—more than I ever could have imagined. Though I had no idea what effect my letters had on the Riveras, to me they became an essential outlet. I was addressing my inner dialogue to Dana.

Another natural consequence of my intense emotional and spiritual connection to the Riveras was my attempt to understand the depth of their loss. It was impossible, but I continued to try to get my head and heart around losing Parker. I woke up in the middle of the night and wondered why our boys were sleeping safely upstairs while Dana and Jim's boy was gone. I would never be able to "get it," but my heart was searching—and aching for Dana.

During my family's dozen years in Ohio, we spent a few weeks each summer back in Texas, off the grid. Our place north of Houston, near New Waverly, is literally at the end of a dirt road that goes nowhere. We would stay in my parents' second home, located a couple of football fields away from my brother's full-time house. Because no one used our house regularly, there was no cable TV and no free Wi-Fi. For many years, the location's remoteness also meant cell phone signals were weak, requiring everyone to stand in a certain location on the back porch to make a call or receive a text. It all added up to loads of extra time for introspection.

The summer of 2015, I spent a lot of that extra thinking time actively trying to understand what Dana's and my connection meant. I can specifically remember writing her during this time and saying that I didn't know what was happening, but it was clearly something special.

As I mulled over our dynamic, attempting to understand why I was compelled to aggressively reach out to the Riveras via old-school mail and pray for them as often as humanly possible, a thought emerged. Perhaps I wasn't behaving irrationally. Maybe the reason my heart was exploding with the Riveras was that a love bigger than mine was happening. What if it was God's love for them that had basically woken me up in the night and dictated that I reach out to Dana?

As I continued to consider this idea, it resonated in a way that made me sure I was on to something. God's love for the Riveras—and specifically Dana—had been inserted into my own human heart. So, while yes, my feelings were my own, God was using my heart, the most powerful entry point, to reach out to the Riveras. Though overwhelming, humbling, and almost ridiculous, it totally made sense to me.

The other thought that kept popping into my head was about the nature of Dana's and my relationship. Everything I knew about her from 1986 to the present was from a series of posts and pictures on the internet. I kept asking myself how a simple Facebook relationship could be so life-changing. If my connection with Dana was so fruitful, I wondered what other untapped goodness existed in my "friends" list.

Finally, I could feel God's love oozing out of every pore of my body, driving me to do something more. While I had no idea what the future held or what this "something" might be, I was certain that I was going to do it. If destiny or fate could be an emotion, this was what it felt like.

I kicked this around in my head for about a week, until one day it came to me: What would happen if I tried to write *all* of my Facebook friends a letter?

July 1-22, 2015

*W*e returned to Ohio in early July—a seventeen-hour car ride. In the front seat by myself, I had all that time to think—about Dana, about God's love, and about my idea to write to my Facebook friends.

I began to formulate a plan: I would set up the project and actually begin writing the letters when I settled back into my other life.

It was a big idea, but, of course, I didn't discuss it with anyone.

Back home, I was thrilled to receive another letter from Dana. It had arrived while I was gone, and was a two-parter written at different times during May.

In it, she answered questions I had about her family, including how she and Jim had gotten to Lafayette. It was also the first time she mentioned all of her daughters by name. Up to that point, my only exposure to them had been what I could glean from Facebook. She also talked about the lost art of letter writing.

> *I miss writing and receiving letters. I plan to have my class write a letter because we have gotten so far away from that! They probably don't even know how! Well, thanks to you, they will. I used to have pen pals for them, but years have gone by and the pressure and standards are different, so pen pals faded, but I will have them write someone before school ends.*

She also detailed the people whom we would eventually call "gappers." That's Dana's word for the people who have stood in the gap with her family between their old and new lives. She didn't provide names, but mentioned an "*awesome* neighbor," a "BFF (from 1982, no less)" and her "teaching BFF, who hangs with me *lots*—she and her husband are our go-to peeps."

I immediately felt compelled to pray for these people, as I understood that they were answers to my prayers. I didn't have to know them personally to be on the same team. From my position of overfeeling, I believed that because they were Dana's people, they were also my people.

Dana wrapped up each letter by thanking me for writing her. Though her endless gratitude always humbled me beyond words, it also spurred me onward. Each word from her served as some sort of validation for me that I wasn't behaving like a freak. Though I was becoming more and more aware of this being God's business, not just mine, I was all wrapped up in it personally. Despite the extraordinary circumstances, I was still just an imperfect person with my own unique set of hang-ups. This meant that I questioned much of what was going on and my place in it. This wasn't how I or "normal" people operated. These people had lost their son, and I was writing them letters, when they didn't even really know who I was. What was I even doing? Yet Dana sent messages like:

I feel blessed to be the recipient of your beautiful words!!
You can't imagine my smile when the envelope arrives.
You are making a difference, my sweet friend!

Love and gratitude,

Dana

It always took me a week or so to transition from Texas back into my life in Ohio. I avoided putting everything away and had to force myself to do anything beyond my writing assignments.

On July 11, I finally got around to putting the first part of my "other" letter-writing campaign into action. Years earlier, I had bought three Stanley desk journals from Levenger—an expensive stationery catalog that I had once been obsessed with. The set included a brown leather cover that held whichever journal was in use.

Of course, I'd never used the journals. One had three pages of a feelings-laden diary I'd tried to start in 2000, and the second and third were still blank. On the drive back to Ohio, I had decided that I would journal about my letter-writing project. Step one was putting the blank journal into the cover and beginning.

The Facebook letters were born of the same passion that compelled me to write Dana. I will always be convinced that I wouldn't have written a single Facebook letter without first reconnecting with the Riveras.

The Facebook Project: Journal Entry #1

"Quite possibly the stupidest idea I ever came up with."
—Amy Daughters

July 11, 2015

When telling the story of Dana Dugas Rivera and the letter-writing campaign I unknowingly went on, one of the most striking parts for me is when I talk about how I initially didn't have her home address, because we were only "Facebook" friends.

So, what is a Facebook friend, and what would happen if I sent each of mine a heartfelt letter via US mail? And can I even find enough to say to fill two pages?

The goal: Write a letter to each of my 512 (verified as of May 13, 2015) FB friends by July 31, 2016. That's approximately 1.4 letters per day.

The rules:

- *Minimum two pages (front and back) each*
- *Research each person first, on FB and other websites.*
- *No unfriending or opting out unless you absolutely don't know the person and have zero mutual friends.*
- *Keep a copy of everything on file and log it all in this notebook.*
- *Ask for addresses if stalking doesn't work. No address = no excuse.*
- *Keep stats in a different notebook.*

Sometimes we hatch a plan that feels so solid, we have no choice but to implement it. Trusting our gut rarely fails us in this kind of scenario, and taking action often changes the whole way we operate, turning thinkers into doers.

Once I became a doer, I couldn't stop. My "keep a copy of everything on file" dictate meant I was planning on literally copying everything I sent out and filing everything that came in. I knew that I would need to make copies because of Dana. In writing her what were nearly thirty letters by that summer, I knew I wasn't going to remember what I said.

What I Think Will Happen

- *I will get some replies via mail and FB but will probably do a poor job of responding. I may resort to messaging back on FB because I'm a crappy pen pal. #ironic*
- *Some people will think it's weird.*
- *I will think it's weird.*
- *It will change my heart.*
- *I will know more about my friends, will care more, and will pray more frequently simply by virtue of treating them like individuals, even if it's just once.*
- *I may not finish.*
- *I will have a hard time writing some of the letters.*
- *It will be awkward.*
- *Like the NordicTrack step climber or Incline, it will be harder than it looks!*

Though I'm not saying this is all definitely God's idea, I do pray for guidance and support and the passion necessary to finish if He's for it.

My explanation of why I was writing, the rules, and my expectations took up the first two pages in the journal. Next came the first two chronological entries:

July 12, 2015

Bought 80 sheets of memo pad stationary on Expressionary.com ($27.30). Will begin when it arrives.

July 13, 2015

Transferred names of 512 FB friends (active) to an Excel spreadsheet.

July 18, 2015

Received stationery/memo pad.

July 20, 2015

Printed Facebook list; cut into strips of paper; put into box.

To hold all the names so I could draw one at a time, I used a small cardboard box. I crudely cut a square hole in the top and wrote, "GOD'S LOVE—this is not about me" on it in purple Sharpie. The words were a direct reflection of my experience with Dana. God's love was what was driving me to write her and pray for her—it really had very little to do with me.

After shoving all the individual names into the little box, a task that made the project seem extremely daunting, I drew the first name and realized, for the first of many times, *Oh, crap—I'm really going to have to write this person a letter.*

Letter #1

Letter #1, to an old camp friend from Texas whom I had known as both a camper and a counselor, was my first "real" Facebook letter—written on the stationery (which had "Amy Weinland Daughters, your Facebook friend" printed at the top of every page) and used the format I would employ for the next 579 letters.

It also established a key practice: I wrote the letter before looking for the recipient's address. This wound up being important because I couldn't use not having an address as an excuse for not writing a specific letter. I was determined to write every single person a letter, whether they received it or not.

July 20, 2015

Dear #1,

Hi! Hope this finds you happy and well. You're probably wondering why I'm writing you a letter. Good question! I have been wondering what being a friend on Facebook is all about—what does it even mean? Then I wondered what it would be like if I tried to write all my FB friends letters, old-school ones, like when we went to camp and college. Would I even have anything to say?

So, anyway, here we are, in letter #1—to you. The last I saw you and your people was at Camp Olympia, with your girls. Are they still attending? I believe you have a son too. Does he go?

Our boys both went first term this summer. Matthew is nine and Will is seventeen, so he was part of O Crew, which is the step between camper and counselor.

Matt will be in the fourth grade this year, and Will will be a senior in high school. We've actually just started doing college visits—Cincinnati, Miami of Ohio, Ohio University, etc. Clearly, we live in Ohio, where my husband's job moved us in 2007.

I do some freelance writing, mostly about college football, on the side, but more than anything, I'm a mom!

I see from your FB page (#stalker) that you went to Northwestern and Duke. That is very cool, I never knew that. The only other Duke alum I know is our mutual friend Mike from camp. Not sure if you remember him and his sister Mary. I saw her at camp when we dropped the kids off.

I would love to hear more about your life in Houston. More than anything, I wanted to express my thanks for your friendship on- and offline. It's interesting that a lot of our FB friendships honor past relationships and experiences. That's a good thing, but it makes me wonder if there's something more than that going on. I want you to know that even if I don't comment or hit "like," or even see everything you post (who knows how that works?), I enjoy seeing you and your people via Facebook. I also want you to know that as your friend, in cyberspace or real life, I care about you and your life. As your friend, I am privileged to pray for and think of you despite the surreal nature of social media.

Thanks for reading this! I look forward to seeing you soon.

Take care and lots of love from your offline friend 4ever,

Amy Weinland Daughters

This very first legitimate "Facebook letter" had many commonalities with all those that came after it.

1. I had to stalk the recipients' FB profiles to find topics to write about. This ended up being one of the biggest upsides of the project: I got to know each of my people better and appreciate them as individuals.

2. I used part of the space to thank the person for their contributions to my life story. This "talk about my feelings" element—a component of almost every letter—led to numerous lightbulb moments. More than anything, I became tremendously more grateful, relationally speaking.

3. The letter has an introduction that I used in other letters as well. The first paragraph of each letter is not only my explanation to the recipient about why they are getting a letter but also a barometer of where I am with the project emotionally. The introduction in this first-ever letter is short, sweet, and far less reflective than other letters' intros. It's also one of the very few that doesn't reference Dana —a relationship and story that was developing while I was starting to write the letters.

4. I refer to the recipient as a "real life" (in this case, "offline") friend. This became my way, I suppose, of transforming the virtual friendship into something actual.

After writing the letter, I searched for #1's address. Since she didn't have obvious employment (the easiest place to mail a random letter), I resorted to asking her outright via the only means I had: a Facebook message. This act turned out to be, repeatedly, even more awkward than writing the letter in the first place. At least I could stick that in the mail and act like it had never happened.

> Hi #1! Hope this finds you well! I know this sounds random, because it probably is, but could I have your address? I wrote you a letter (for real) and want to send it to you! Take care and all the best, Amy

I hit SEND, put my phone where I couldn't see it, and tried to go about my business like I hadn't just established a new level of ridiculousness. Unbelievably, #1 replied, providing her full address, within the hour. It was one of the top ten most shocking moments in the history of the project.

I'll never completely understand why people—to whom, for the most part, I hadn't spoken to in decades—so willingly gave me their physical addresses. In this era when social media is rampant, there's still no substitute for direct communication and personal touches.

I made a copy of letter #1 and mailed it that same day. I wrote the letter number and the recipient's address on the copy. Finally, I taped the recipient's name, the little slip of paper I had pulled from the box, onto the bottom of the copied letter. All three were tasks I would repeat with every subsequent letter I wrote.

A mere four days after I mailed the letter, I received my first reply, via Facebook messenger:

> July 24, 2015
>
> Amy—you made my week!! I plan to write back ASAP (good

luck reading my handwriting) but just wanted you to know
how touched I was to receive your letter. What a nice idea.
Have a great weekend, and you will receive a letter back soon.
That just made me so happy. ☺
Best,
#1

The next week, I received a handwritten letter from #1. It
was the first-ever Facebook letter to arrive in *my* mailbox! Other
than being a historic moment, it raised the question of what I
was going to do in terms of answering replies.

I marked in the journal the need for a reply, which I labeled
"Reply #1A." I responded to #1's reply on August 17, in actual
letter form on my FB stationery, and then attached to the initial
letter a copy of everything I already had on file. This was one of
only two responses I'd do in writing. From the third reply onward, I answered letters using my vintage typewriter and a set of
telegrams I had purchased on Etsy but never used. It was an al-
ternate form of old-school communication that didn't require
me to write by hand and allowed me to be brief.

My decision to respond to #1's written reply was significant
because it set a precedent that if people responded to my letter in
writing, I intended to attempt to respond in kind. Not only
would this become an ongoing challenge, but I would end up
feeling guilty when I ultimately couldn't do so.

Two elements of #1's written response were common threads
that were eventually woven into many of the responses I received
in the future. First, #1 reflected on social media and how it affects our relationships. Many times, these observations would be
profound, providing keen insight into what the internet has
done to redefine the term "friendship."

I do love FB in that it has helped me reconnect with so many friends from long ago. You are right that it is an interesting question to wonder what those relationships mean. I think that as we get older, we think more about these things and the importance of connections.

Next, #1 mentioned the timing of the letter. A recipient's claim that their letter arrived at just the right moment would also be repeated again and again. It fascinated me because I was just randomly pulling names out of a box.

I have always believed in timing. Two of my kids recently both read a fabulous book about an American girl and a boy in Zimbabwe and the pen pal relationship they developed over a period of years. My kids wanted pen pals after that, so they are both now writing letters to kids abroad. As they have been doing that, I have thought about how little I write people anymore. Your timing was perfect!

Letter #5

Letter #5 was to my brother's wife. She was the very first family member I wrote to. Communications to this group allowed me to say all those little and big things that go unsaid when you're busy doing life together—the thoughts and feelings that are in your head and on your heart, but that you don't ever get a chance to express because you have no forum in which to do so. Though I hadn't expected it, these letters allowed me to tick more boxes that I had never known existed. As it turns out, I needed to write them.

Since I hadn't yet shared the project with anyone, this was also our wider family's introduction to it.

July 27, 2015

Dear #5,

Well, of course you are now asking yourself why I am sending you a letter. That's a great question. Welcome to my little Facebook project, where I try to write each of my friends an actual letter. I am doing this because of what I have learned from writing my friend Dana in Louisiana, namely how I didn't have her home address because she was "just a Facebook friend." That got me thinking, what is a Facebook friend and what does it even mean? What, if anything, do I have to say to these people?

Drawing your name from the five hundred–plus possibilities obviously was greeted with a sigh of relief by me, as it delayed a potentially awkward page-and-a-half musing about my past and present.

Anyway, I am thankful for this opportunity to express some feelings in writing. These are not, by the way, done in honor of FB.

First, I want you to know how glad I am that you married my beloved brother and that you specifically were chosen to be the mother of his and your children, my beloved nieces and nephews. I know that many people may think, and perhaps express to you, how lucky you are to have married into the Weinland family. Though there are definite upsides to "us," I want you to know that even I can see the potential pitfalls, such as Let's not discuss anything that's real, Let's just assume and expect that everyone automatically understands the rules of engagement, and Let's not go to each other directly when addressing the group with a problem is preferred. On that note, I want to thank you for putting up with us.

I believe your honesty and love and grace have made <u>all of us</u> a stronger, tighter unit. And, I believe the hard work you've put in, especially in one-on-one relationships like ours, make us a viable, wonderful entity moving forward.

Above all, please know that I respect and love you very much. I admire your strength, your humor, your creativity, and your overwhelming desire to serve others and treat them to things beyond their wishes. By this, I don't just mean "stuff"—although you're definitely good at that. I mean you create unique experiences as well. You have a gift of seeing people's hearts! And these emotions transcend your role as my sister-in-law; I love and respect you separately from your place in our family.

I so look forward to all the memories we have yet to make.

It's going to be a scary, interesting, awkward, hilarious, joyous, tragic, and wonderful ride. I'm just thankful we'll be sitting near each other, with our phones, for the entire journey.

Love from your sister and friend.

It's a good letter—even I'll admit that. The mistake would be giving me the credit. Though I wrote the words and they're mine, it's God's love that inspired them in the first place. It's God's love for Dana and her family, layered with my love for my own people.

My sister-in-law responded to my letter via text message almost three weeks after I wrote it. It was one of the most significant responses I'd receive in the entire project.

August 14, 2015

I received your "Facebook letter" and was flabbergasted (that's a cool word to type). I was so much so that the letter I am writing back to you has said "Dear Amy" for over a week now. So maybe I shall text you how much I appreciated your sentiments and how thankful I am for our friendship in this walk-through life. Very thankful! I realize words are a way you show love and are your preferred medium, so I felt that a text was a little inferior to putting pen to paper, and then I finally realized that when someone goes to the lengths you did, you might like some positive feedback! Keep trucking with those letters, Amy! A good idea and very well received. Almost so nice that the recipient can feel a little not worthy of all the nice words. Maybe that's just if I'm the recipient! It might be true of others, so don't think that your words aren't life to

someone and aren't well received if they don't quite know how
to respond. You are loved and respected and enjoyed by all
who know you.

"Don't think that your words aren't life to someone and aren't well received if they don't quite know how to respond." That statement set the tone for how I approached my expectations for responses not just to the letters, but to so many areas of my regular life. It is one of the most important, far-reaching things anyone has ever said to me.

As humans, we are wired to anticipate a response from someone we reach out to. Electronic, instantaneous communication—which allows our words to be read immediately—heightens the expectation for a response.

My sister-in-law's words encouraged me not to get caught up in who did and didn't reply to the letters. She reminded me that individuals are equipped very differently. Where one person could and would respond eloquently and immediately, it would equally be impossible for another to do so. What *wouldn't* fluctuate was the potential impact each letter could have.

We don't need a response to validate that we've made a difference.

Letter #7

The recipient of letter #7 was the wife of one of Willie's work associates, who also just so happened to be the older sister of one of my brother's best friends. We saw each other at least a couple of times a year, and though we weren't in contact regularly, we gravitated to each other in a way that almost felt like family.

July 28, 2015

Dear #7,

Hi! Hope this finds you happy and well. You're probably wondering why I'm writing you a letter. Good question! Recently, I began to wonder about being friends on Facebook—what is it all about, and what does it even mean? And if I tried, could I write each of my FB friends a letter?

So, here we are, in a letter to you, my FB friend, and thankfully my friend in real life as well.

When I think about you, I can't help but be amazed at all our many connections: We grew up in the same neighborhood, our brothers played in a band together in high school and are still friends, our sisters-in-law are close, and our nieces and nephews often play together. Then, on top of all of that, our husbands work together, and therefore we have another set of mutual friends! So, while we've never really "hung out" on a consistent basis, you are everywhere I look and we are very connected.

I must say, I think I've done well and got lucky that it

was you, rather than some fruitcake, that I got connected with!

Please know that though I might not "like" all of your FB business, I like you and consider your friendship and our connection a blessing. One of the gifts of this FB project is that I've been afforded the opportunity to appreciate, think about, and pray for the people I call "friend." Know that I feel lucky to count you among this group.

See you on- and offline soon!

Love,

Amy

Your FB and real-life friend ☺

Though #7 responded via a Facebook message in early August, she didn't reply in writing until early the next year.

February 14, 2016

Finding a letter in the mailbox, holding an envelope and pages purposely addressed to and written to me, was a nice treat. The deliberateness of a letter cannot be translated on FB. The words are more honest, believable, and genuine than social media could ever be. Quirky and concise don't carry the same warmth.

While our "posts" and "comments" on social media can spawn honest and meaningful discourse between two individuals, they are public. Knowing that the rest of our friends list (and our friends' friends) can see what we're saying naturally changes our tone and message. That's just human nature.

In addition, the way to deliver an influential message on social media seems to be to do it in as few words as possible. Though this brevity may pack more of a punch, that kind of exchange between two individuals can squeeze out meaning.

Reaching out to someone outside social media, even electronically, is entirely different because it's 100 percent private and personal. And an old-school letter is next-level because it's noninstantaneous and intentional in a way that lets the recipient know that the writer values them enough to sacrifice time and effort for them.

What a letter could mean to people in the age of social media was something I had no clue about until I began writing the letters.

The other significant observation #7 made is how delicious it is to hold in your hand something that your friend has also held—something they intended just for you, something that has no monetary value but has personal worth beyond measure.

Letter #10

Letter #10 was to a guy I'd known and loved in high school but hadn't spoken to since. I knew from his posts that we didn't share the same political views. I was more on the conservative spectrum—especially fiscally—while he was more liberal. Given that I wrote to him before the 2016 presidential election cycle, the gap between our approaches was even more distinct. We also had different lifestyles: I was a married, stay-at-home, heterosexual mom and part-time writer in suburban Ohio; he was a single, homosexual man with a full-time career living in a metropolitan area of Southern California.

Here's what love—not me or my words—did to shrink the differences between us.

August 10, 2015

First, let me say that I remember you fondly (I mean that) from KOHS. I admit that my memories of high school are not the greatest. Sure, there was good stuff, but I wasted a lot of it feeling insecure and like I didn't fit in. Then there was you. I remember eating lunch with you and how friendly and funny you were. Maybe we weren't best friends, but you definitely made things better for me.

Next up, I've always wanted to tell you (and again, I mean this wholeheartedly) that I respect your posts, commentary, and shares on FB. Though I may not agree 100 percent with everything you put out there, I respect it and the level of intelligence that you offer with each item. I also think you are incredibly brave to stick to your beliefs, especially given our shared experience in the rigid box of a suburban Texan upbringing. Honestly, I find myself wanting more and more to bust out of said box, establishing my own set of beliefs and standards that can't be labeled by a religious or political party designation. Overall, thanks for keeping it real.

Letter #10 was the first time I signed with "Your friend in REAL life." I would repeat this addition under my signature in almost all of the 570 letters I had left to write.

Two weeks after I wrote him, the recipient of Letter #10 sent me a response via Facebook Messenger.

August 24, 2015

Reading your letter made me feel good about my life, what I've done, what I'm doing, and what I still have left to do.

This was another pivotal moment early in the project. Reaching across the proverbial aisle and being honest with someone I didn't have a lot of obvious connection points with elicited what might have been the greatest response in the entire endeavor.

The recurring theme that Letter #10 illustrated was that other people's words—in response to my own words—were going to change me more than I ever could have imagined.

I didn't set out to transform anyone's heart (including my own) by writing the letters; I simply acted on what I felt driven to do. This lack of intention made the results—especially those that manifested into my own feelings—seem almost magical.

September 2015

*A*s I continued chipping away at my project, I received a letter from Dana dated Tuesday, September 15. It was National Childhood Cancer Awareness Month, and many of her Facebook posts had revolved around raising awareness and money for that cause. Cleverly, she used pictures and described personal experiences to introduce special staff members and even specific departments at St. Jude.

Her September 4 post was one of the hardest to read. It was the eight-month anniversary of Parker's death.

> Seems like hours, yet it is eight months today. I still find myself shocked at moments. So today's post will be about where we started and ended our St. Jude journey. I will start with the end and, if I have a chance this month, go back to the beginning.
>
> Parker was admitted to the ICU on a Friday. We met Dr. Sam, the hospitalist, who (thank you, Lord) was on the floor that weekend. Specialists from around Memphis were called in all through the night. Parker coded Friday night, and the entire hospital, it seemed, came running. They were able to save him, and I know he waited because Alli, Peyton, and Jacque were on their way to Memphis. Jim, Lauren, Mady, and I huddled in a corner of the room while Lauren led us in prayer—words that

only the Holy Spirit could've come up with. Parker was given thirty-plus transfusions, platelets . . . I do believe Dr. Sam was giving us time! What other hospital would do all that? Saturday we painted with him (I know he was aggravated because he wasn't a painter type) and listened to Johnny Cash —his favorite! We had a beautiful day and told him everything we wanted to say. Someone was holding his hands and stroking his hair every second. On Sunday, our nurse came back wearing her Johnny Cash shirt—it was actually a shirt Parker had too ☺.

When it was time, we told him it was okay, we loved him, and we would see him again! ICU can be scary, but St. Jude ICU NEVER GAVE UP, and when they knew where we were headed, they gave us TIME to spend and make beautiful memories. We will be forever grateful for that! #TEAMPARKER #STJUDEMEMPHISMARATHON #RAISINGMONEY ☺

I was at my desk when I read Dana's words. I immediately went over to the now-well-used chair in the corner and prayed crazily. I didn't even know what to ask God for. "Only you know what she needs," I pleaded. "I'm just going to kneel down here in silence and focus on you delivering precisely what she needs precisely when she needs it."

Eventually I went back to my desk and sat down. I physically felt for Dana—I could never understand the depth of her grief, but somehow, I had a deep pain in my own chest.

The phone rang, breaking the silence. The caller ID said ST. JUDE.

No lie.

When I answered, the caller identified herself as a fundraiser. As it was National Childhood Cancer Awareness Month, she wanted to know if I would consider increasing my monthly donation. We had been giving monthly to St. Jude for several years after a neighbor on our street did a campaign.

Um, yes, I'll triple my donation. Absolutely.

Regardless of what the lady on the phone believed or didn't believe, God had just called me directly using her phone line.

I shared the story that next Sunday when I wrote Dana. As always, I was hesitant with my words, worried that I was going to say something the wrong way. I wanted desperately for the letters to be positive; the last thing I wanted my words to do was to make things worse or offend.

I sent off the letter, hoping for the best. It was something I would experience over and over again—trusting God but not trusting God.

The first paragraph of her latest reply was a relief.

Amy:

Your last letter floored me! My Facebook posts had taken an emotional toll on me, so I took a break. Peyton is on homecoming court, and it worked out that I could invest all my Facebook energy in her! I have much more to share and people I want to discuss and introduce to the world, but I was considering backing off after this week—still posting for Children's Cancer Month, but maybe just some statistics. The love and feedback have been uplifting, but just wasn't sure I could do it. Then your letter came! Your beautiful words have inspired me, so my posts will continue at least for the last week or two of September. THANK YOU!

It was insanity. I was reading Dana's Facebook posts, saying prayers that no one knew anything about (except for God), and then responding to her in writing (as if it were 1983). This bizarre combination—somehow, some way—was resulting in mind-blowing stuff that was *actually happening*. And somehow we were using old-school communication (handwritten letters) combined with new-age technology (free long distance and Facebook), and everyone's heart was changing.

This crap was for real.

Maybe, just maybe, we can't comprehend even half of what is really going on all around us.

Letter #21

I went through most of school with #21 and sat next to him at high school graduation. When I wrote to him, he was suffering through major health issues. I knew this not because I was in regular contact with him but because of updates he had posted on Facebook. What I didn't know were the details. The letter gave me the opportunity both to ask him for more information and to tell him that I was thinking about him and sincerely cared about what was happening.

If my project hadn't forced me to write this letter, I would have never gotten engaged in #21's story. In other words, I could have cared silently, but now I was going to have to care out loud.

September 5, 2015

Dear #21,

Greetings! You're probably wondering why I'm writing you a letter. Good question! Recently, I started wondering what being friends on Facebook is all about. What does it even mean? Are there rules or requirements? What are we supposed to do? Then I got a crazy idea and wondered if I could manage to write each of my five hundred–plus Facebook friends an actual letter. Would I even have anything to say?

That brings us here, to your letter. What's interesting about you specifically is that I actually feel like I know you better because of FB. Yes, we went to high school together. Yes, we even sat next to each other at graduation. And yes, we've even seen each other recently, something I certainly can't say about 75 percent of my FB people. But, all that aside, it's your posts that make me know you, because you are willing to share more than pictures of your cats and inspirational quotes.

Here is some of what I know:

1. You like the Texans and football (YAY for that!).

2. You have a beautiful daughter.

3. You are passionate about food and cooking.

4. You have been job hunting.

5. You have recently suffered some major health concerns.

But even though I know these things and am glad to know them, I have questions—stuff I should know but don't.

Here are but a few questions:

1. How old is your daughter? What are her aspirations for the future?

2. What specifically happened to you medically? Are you okay now?

3. Are you working now? I mean, I see that you have an employer listed on FB, but I'm not sure if it's current. For example, mine says I work in packaging at Dairy Queen....

More than anything, I want you to know that I care about you and hope (really, for reals) that all is well. Though I didn't say it (and should have), I prayed for you when I saw your posts about your health. And I hope you continue to gain strength and are able to re-create your life in a way that provides you with maximum happiness.

Take care, my friend. I look forward to seeing you on FB and perhaps again in real life!

Lots of love,

Amy W. D.

Your friend in REAL life

Number 21 responded via handwritten letter just two weeks after I wrote him.

September 21, 2015

Amy,

I was very pleased to receive your letter! It's nice to know that someone sees my posts on FB ☺. My beautiful daughter is almost fifteen, attends a prep school, runs cross-country/track, plays volleyball, will play basketball, and loves history and science. I've raised her alone since she was four, as her mother had a drug addiction.

After I had my car wreck last year (and shattered my spine), my daughter had to move back in with her mother in Austin, who has been sober for five years. I had a massive seizure after surgery, which cost me my driver's license and forced me to move back to Houston.

I've been employed locally for a month now, but my goal is Austin! Austin by January! My baby needs me! I appreciate your prayers and want to say I'm able to walk, run, lift stuff, etc., now. Good prayer you had!

Thanks for the letter and the wake-up call.

See you again,

#21

Recipient #21's reply illustrated an angle of social media that I would be reminded of again and again throughout the project: What you see on Facebook isn't an accurate depiction of "real" life.

Number 21 came across as happy and opinionated online. Though he did mention his health issues and that he had a daughter, his news feed could never properly express the depth of his struggle. You had to go deeper to get to that. And that's precisely what I did—by writing a letter that I would never have written without the Facebook project.

He closed his response by saying he was off to write the girl who sat on the other side of him at graduation a letter. It was one of the single funniest lines in the history of the project.

It took me just shy of two months to reply to #21. The timing of that would haunt me forever. During those sixty days, his health deteriorated, and he passed away on November 16, in Tomball, Texas; he was only forty-seven.

I had replied via telegram to his handwritten response to my original letter (written September 4) on November 13, which was a Friday. Even if I had mailed it that day, which was unlikely, the earliest he would have received it in Texas would have been the 17th or 18th.

It meant that I had missed him by only days.

```
Dear #21,

Greetings. Sorry it has taken me so long to
reply to your card. I wanted to let you know
that of all the responses I have received to
my Facebook letters, your quip about
"writing a letter to the girl who sat on the
other side of [you] at high school
graduation, as she was always behind [you]"
was by far the best and funniest so far.
```

```
Thanks for that.

Please also know that we are all praying for
you and looking forward to your health
returning completely. You are truly loved by
those lucky enough to call you a friend.

Lots of love and best wishes,

Amy Daughters

Your friend on Facebook and in real life
```

Though other Facebook friends of mine would pass away during the project, #21 would be the only one who would die during a period of active communication. I have often wondered if his family read my reply sometime after his passing but were unaware of the rest of the story.

As much as #21's death shocked and saddened me, and as much as I regretted not having sent the telegram sooner, I was also thankful that we had reconnected at all. I had had the opportunity to tell him, in a one-on-one setting, that I cared.

If you get the urge to do something, do it. You never know when it might be too late.

Letter #49

Though I couldn't have known it at the time, the story of letter #49 would eventually become one of the most compelling to result from the Facebook project.

Number 49 was a close high school friend. We lost touch after college but reconnected on Facebook. We also saw each other during the brief time when I lived in Houston between England and Ohio. It meant that our relationship went beyond "just online," because we had each other's cell numbers, but really, we were seeing nothing more than what was on the surface.

Though I had friends and enjoyed parts of my high school experience, I was still struggling with low self-confidence and the issues with my mom. Number 49 lived through the epicenter of this with me. Now, thirty years later, in a random letter, I had a chance to reflect on all of it.

November 10, 2015

One of the real upsides of this little project has been the opportunity to say things, in horrible handwriting, to special people who are both in my life and on FB. It's stuff I should have already said, but I am blessed with the opportunity to do so now, as an unforeseen benefit of what initially seemed like a ridiculous endeavor.

In your case, I feel so thankful for your friendship, both the version that stretches back and the one today. In both forms, you are one of the most supportive, loving friends I have ever had.

When I think back to high school, I realize what a hot

mess I was, truly. We all had a lot going on back then, and I know I was not alone in feeling lost, but boy, was I. What I needed, I suppose, was to feel loved and cared for —something we all need no matter how old we are. And that's where you came bouncing into the story— prepared, somehow, to be my friend and advocate, despite my awkwardness.

How big a deal was it? You helped me and were one of the primary reasons I survived high school. I know you know this, but I really struggled with my relationship with my mom, especially while you and I were close. Before I left home, I didn't realize how messed up it was, but you got me through it and to the other side.

You showed me firsthand how love and grace work. Honestly, I'm not sure how you thank somebody for that, but please know that you have made the biggest difference in my life, and that where I am now—happy, confident, and mostly whole—has so much to do with your love and friendship.

If you ever ask yourself, "What have I done? or, "Is anything making a difference?" go—right now—and look yourself in the mirror and tell yourself, "You saved someone's life" and, "Yes! You change lives."

I am blessed and overwhelmingly thankful to be your friend.

Love you 4ever,

Amy W. D.

Your friend in REAL life

Number 49's reply, four handwritten pages, was emotional, not just because she was replying to my feelings-laden letter but because she was still close friends with the recipient of letter #21, our high school friend who passed away. Her letter was dated November 20, which meant she wrote it just four days after he died.

November 28, 2015

I received your beautiful letter. It could not have come at a more perfect time. I am grieving our sweet friend's death, and the holidays are upon us. . . .

Number 49 also offered some beautiful commentary on how God puts people in our lives. Her words foreshadowed one of the primary lessons I learned from Dana and the Facebook project—namely, that relationships don't happen by coincidence.

Something else I've recently learned is that the Lord divinely places people in our lives at very specific and purposeful moments. He knows what we need and precisely when we need it—or them. He created us. Our lives are like a symphony with many instruments. Sometimes you need the violins, while other times only a tuba will do. Ha ha!

Even more important than her words was the fact that the line of communication that was now open between #49 and me would continue to build toward something bigger.

February 6, 2016

On this date, my Facebook friend Nicole took her own life. I had grown up with her and remained connected with her through Facebook. She was also best friends, in 2016, with #49.

Her suicide, which came about seven months into the project, was a major turning point in my letter writing.

Nicole was a dynamic person. She was involved in politics but never demeaned anyone who held an opposing view and never spoke in hate. She was an exception to social media's increasingly volatile and politicized culture.

I had looked forward to the day when I would draw her name out of the box. I felt like she was one of the few people who would totally appreciate what I was trying to do.

I was determined now more than ever to complete this project. Not only did Nicole's death make my letter writing feel more urgent, but it made me want to express my thanks and love to people whose life paths had beautifully intersected with my own. We shouldn't ever hesitate to share gratitude when we feel it.

My journal entry three days after Nicole's suicide connected the dots between her, #49, and the Facebook letters.

February 9, 2016

I can't get Nicole out of my mind. In telling the story of #49 calling me with the news, I realized that the reason she called me so quickly was probably the FB letters— meaning yes, we had already reconnected, mostly via text, but the exchange via letter was so meaningful that she thought to reach out to me because she needed a friend who cared. That's powerful shit.

It seems obvious to say people need love and to be cared

for. But they do—for real. Like, maybe Maslow's Hierarchy of Needs needs to be amended, so that love and friendship become as critical as food, water, and shelter, or perhaps just beneath those items but before cars and candles.

I suppose what I'm doing here with the letters is important, but it's also a daunting emotional commitment, not only to myself but to all these people I'm writing and telling I care. It's a promise that shouldn't be made loosely or without forethought. Words mean something, but they don't. In the same way, this endeavor is everything, but it is also nothing. That's like life, I suppose.

My heart breaks for Nicole. RIP, friend.

Nicole and #49 had known each other in high school and had gone on to become BFFs in adult life. Whereas for me, Nicole's passing was my old friend ending her life, for #49 it meant that her "person" had ended it all suddenly.

Notably, I was the third phone call #49 made. It's something I credited at the time to our renewed communication from the Facebook project. I realized that while I likely would have heard about Nicole quickly, I wouldn't have been that high up on the list without the letters. This circumstance illustrated, once again, how powerful personal, one-on-one communication is, especially in the world of social media.

I came off the phone that day utterly shocked about Nicole and deeply concerned about #49. What happened next was a combination of what I had already learned from Dana's and my pen-palling and the Facebook letters. On the one hand, I realized that though I couldn't really do anything for #49, I could choose not to move on. On the other, I understood that I had to live up to the emotional promises of love and friendship I had offered #49 in our in-writing communication.

So I began texting her every single evening, checking in, telling her I was praying for her and that she wasn't alone. This would continue for the next eight months.

During our annual time in Texas that summer, #49 came and visited me at our remote family place. I had been excited about her visit, though somewhat hesitant, as it had been so long since we had seen each other in person and so much had happened to her recently. I knew she wasn't in a good place.

She arrived late in the afternoon on one day and planned on leaving the next morning. She brought alcohol with her (which added to what I already had in the house) and even got us each a fun wineglass to drink out of. I was alone, so the consumption plan worked well for me.

The evening started out fun. She was the same old #49—headstrong, confident, opinionated, transparent, and fun—and the mood was celebratory. I drove her around the property, and we ate dinner with my brother—whom she hadn't seen since the late '80s—and his family. After that, we returned across the field to my parents' second home, where I always stayed during our visits.

As the night progressed, the drinking continued. Red wine was the drink of choice, so our sobriety declined rapidly. I couldn't keep up, not because I didn't want to, but because I physically couldn't. Additionally, I did get a sense—in the form of some little "ping" in my brain—that I should try to stay in control of myself.

So, I slowed down while #49 kept going. We discussed a lot

of things, and we got deep. Inevitably, as midnight neared, we broached the subject of Nicole's death. She gave me a blow-by-blow of how it all happened. It was ugly.

As the hours rolled on, #49 began to spin out of control, going from what was almost a state of uncontrollable rage to a state of total emotional breakdown. She'd aggressively yell at me, argue with every point I made, call me names, and then repeatedly insert herself into my arms, sobbing. She even kissed my shoulder at one point.

"You're one of the best friends I've ever had in my entire life," she whispered, curled up on my lap.

Regardless of which way her emotions swung, she continued to circle back to a common theme. When she calmed, she pontificated on the certainty of the existence of God. When her anger heightened, she took the opposite approach.

"The Devil is real!" she screeched.

It was this phrase that she repeated, over and over again, as well as belaboring the point that she didn't understand why Nicole had taken her own life. Number 49 had just spoken to her. Nicole had two beautiful children and a husband who loved her. Number 49 couldn't get the picture of Nicole's suicide out of her head. Why hadn't Nicole told #49 that she was on the edge?

"I could have helped her if I had known," she sobbed.

By 2:00 a.m., I was emotionally exhausted and didn't know if I could go on. I actually considered leaving her there in my parents' house. I'm not sure where I would have gone, but I wanted to walk out—this despite the fact that I was acutely aware that she was in the throes of horrific grief and believed she was in a "safe" place with me. She needed this.

But I no longer wanted to be safe. I just wanted to go to bed. And cry. And turn off the show that was playing out in front of me.

We finally went to bed at around 3:00 a.m., after I'd spent an hour suggesting that should happen.

The next morning, thankfully, we didn't discuss what had occurred in the wee hours of the night.

"Thank you for listening," she told me before she left to drive back home.

"I'm glad you told me what you did," I responded, a half-truth that left me feeling even more guilty.

Two days after #49 left, I was still feeling the aftershocks of her visit, so I turned to my journal to try to make sense of it.

June 17, 2016

Is this what reconnecting—for real—looks like?

What does it mean—really—when I tell people I care (which I sincerely do—even if I don't know them well)? Does it open me up too far? Further than I'm willing to go?

Another thought: Is this what a real relationship looks like? In other words, is this authentic because it's not "just a Facebook person" anymore and instead is real—meaning hugely good and terribly bad?

Is my reaction to #49 a gauge of how out of whack my concept of a "relationship" is—i.e., I'm "friends" with these people, but only for the glossy, good stuff?

While I don't think I'll ever be able to answer those questions with absolute certainty, I do know that there are risks (emotional and otherwise) associated with engaging in "real" relationships. Hundreds of letters and several years later, I have

also come to believe not only that it is worth the gamble to participate in one-on-one relationships, but that the instances that
seem the trickiest are also the ones that have the most potential
to change us.

Of all the lessons I learned from the Facebook project, #49's
impact may have been the most powerful. Our words mean
something. We need to be prepared to follow through on what
we promise, because we may be called upon to do so.

Letter #65

Letter #65 was to a camp friend whom I had known since we were younger. We had been both campers and counselors at the same time. We had also seen each other at least once at the alumni reunions Olympia held every two years. We had a large group of mutual friends and many shared memories, and I had always admired #65, who was beautiful and successful, but we had never been super close one-on-one. I almost felt as if she was "out of my league" as a friend.

November 30, 2015

Dear #65,

Hi, friend! Hope this finds you and your family all happy and well. First things first: So, why am I writing you an actual, old-school letter? That's a very good question, especially given my poor spelling and highly offensive handwriting. How delighted I was when I pulled your name from the box—my camp friend whom I still know and love. Please know that it is with excitement and a big smile on my face that I pen this letter to you.

When I think about you, I love, love, love that I'm not sure precisely when we met. Think about that: How many friends do you have whom you have known so long that you don't really know when it all started? You are one of those people for me, and it's a true gift. I feel so fortunate to have known you all these years and am thankful for camp reunions and, yes, Facebook, for keeping us in touch. I love seeing you and your beautiful family and

*am in awe of the fact that you birthed four children!
Please know that actual humans look at your photos and
posts and enjoy them both.*

*That said, I look at your profile and find that I still have
questions—like, how old are these four kids? Where do
they go to school? How did you meet the tall delight that
is your husband? Where in Houston do you live? Who
from camp are you still in close contact with?*

*As for us, we've been in Ohio (forty-five minutes north of
Cincinnati) since 2007, and while it's clearly NOT Texas,
we do love it. Will is a high school senior (eighteen), and
Matthew is in fourth grade. Will just got accepted to Ohio
University and is still waiting to hear back from Miami
(of Ohio) and the University of Cincinnati. The process of
college applications is a world unto itself. . . . #wow I'm at
home and still freelance writing on the side. Overall, it's
amazing, frustrating, thrilling, boring, tragic, and
joyous. In other words, it's REAL life. Yay for that, and
OMG, this is crazy!*

*All in all, I hope you know how much I value all our
many connections and your friendship both on- and
offline. I have always respected the way you carry yourself
and the grace and love you show others. Honestly, you
bring the legit meter on my friends list up an entire notch
(or two). I care deeply for you and for your family and
will keep you all in my prayers.*

Take care, #65 ☺!

Lots of love,

Amy W. D.

Your friend in REAL life

What she said in her reply, via Facebook message, totally took me by surprise.

December 19, 2015

Thank you sooooo much for my amazing letter. I loved it! I loved that it was an old-fashioned written letter, and I loved that it was from you. I never really thought you liked me at camp, let alone that you had thought of me since. I loved hearing about you being a mom and having the same trials in Ohio that I have here, and I love knowing that you are still writing and charming the world with your sense of humor. Thank you!

I would never have guessed in a million years that #65 got the feeling that I didn't like her when we were at camp together. Inasmuch as I truly felt bad about that, I was glad she told me. That level of honesty made me realize that as sure as I was about so much of my past, I had no clue how I had come across to other people—in both good and bad ways.

Her response also illustrated another major lesson I learned from the Facebook project: Perception works both ways. So, as much as I had my assumptions about #65, she had hers as well. In both cases, a portion thereof was based on our actual history, and some came via what we saw on social media.

Frankly, I was somewhat intimidated by #65 during our in-person time because she was gorgeous and smart and seemed to have it all together. To her, this came across as my disliking her. If that's not a life-changing observation, I don't know what is.

Letter #66

⚭

Letter #66 highlights another set of recurring themes I encountered when writing the Facebook letters. First, the recipient was somebody I felt super awkward writing to. Second, because I didn't really know the person, I would never, ever have expected to hear back from her.

I met #66, a twentysomething-year-old, at my college roommate's daughter's wedding. This placed her among my loosest Facebook connections. The potential awkwardness of this category of recipients—people whom I had known in person only very briefly because of a common friend—wasn't something I thought to be wary of going into the project.

The opening paragraphs of my letter illustrate just how tenuous my personal relationship with #66 was and how my explanation about why I was writing the letters was continuing to evolve.

December 1, 2015

Dear #66,

Greetings! First things first: I hope you remember me, in real life, from Molly's wedding. To reintroduce myself, in horrible handwriting, I am Nancy's Texas Tech roommate and friend for life Amy Daughters.

So, why in the world am I writing you a letter, on paper, after meeting you at a wedding several years ago? That's a really good question. Recently, I've been wondering what being friends on Facebook is all about. What does it even mean? It all started when I wanted to write a FB friend a

*few supportive cards as her son was battling cancer. After
I wrote the first one, I realized I didn't know where to
send it. I didn't have her address because, well, she was
"just a Facebook friend." That got me thinking: What is
the difference between "real people" and "just FB" people,
or, instead, are they all the same, only I treat them or
approach them differently? Then I got really ridiculous
and wondered what would happen if I wrote each and
every one of my FB friends a letter. Would I even have
anything to say? How many addresses would I have to
ask for? Would it be the most awkward thing ever?*

Since I thought I'd never hear back from #66, I was aston-
ished when I received her handwritten reply five months later.

April 25, 2016

*I'll just be 100 percent honest: I'm embarrassed that it
took me this long to respond, when I was so excited and
amazed that you wrote me. It was so fun to get a
handwritten letter, especially because it meant something
deeper. I actually thought I would write you back way
sooner, but it felt like life got crazy, and honestly, the
further I got away from the day I received your letter, the
less I wanted to write back because I felt embarrassed. . . .*

This kind of delayed response time was another common
thread in the project. First, so many people who responded to
my letter electronically mentioned that they were planning an
in-writing reply. Of these, only a small percentage ultimately
mailed back a written response.

Next, of the in-writing responses I received, so many began

with "I can't believe how long it took me to write you back." This was also something *I said* in most of my telegram responses to in-writing replies.

It's important to point out that I really did have zero expectations about responses. While yes, I *loved* hearing back from friends, it wasn't something that was making it or breaking it for me.

I came to believe that there must be a certain profile for the people who responded in writing—something in their DNA or the way they were hardwired. It wasn't that the people who responded were "better" than the ones who didn't; it's more that they were born with different character traits.

I really wanted the responses to be a reflection of who truly wanted to reply, as opposed to those who felt obligated. It meant that I tried to never, ever ask a recipient if they were going to write me back. That would have skewed the statistical results of the project. As a numbers girl, I wasn't having any of that.

All of this made #66's response even more noteworthy. She did write back, despite the delay. And if she hadn't, she wouldn't have provided one of the more astute observations on social media to come out of the project:

> *How funny that we are all so in tune with Facebook posts, updates, etc., yet I really do not know deeply most of the people I am "friends" with there. God has been reminding me to slow down, not because FB is bad or useless, but because we are connected without ever needing to invest.*

In the commodity of relationships, investing means depositing something of personal value into another human to achieve a richer connection with them.

This transaction isn't required for "friendships" on Facebook because they exist in a realm where personal investment is impossible. We simply can't sacrifice our time, our patience, our grace, our goals, our privacy, or even our freedom in our online relationships. It's not that we don't want to give up such things to those we like and even love online; it's that the surreal nature of social media makes doing so an impossibility. Investing happens only one-on-one, personally, in "real" life.

Where Facebook certainly has value and keeps us in touch, it doesn't allow us to experience the hope and fear associated with risking a part of our very selves for a relationship.

December 2015

*T*he fall of 2015 marked the birth of another idea for my in-writing, in-prayer relationship with Dana.

I had continued to share the Riveras' story among my close friends and family. In doing so, I always asked the person to join me in praying for Dana and Jim and their girls. In the letters themselves, I continued to discuss #CONSTANT prayer—reminding Dana every week that she had people praying for her around the clock. It made me think about prayer all the time. Not only was I compelled to lift up the Riveras more and more frequently, I spent time considering how prayer worked.

First, I realized that the people I knew were a very small subset of a bigger group that was praying for Dana and Jim. Though we didn't even know 95 percent of the team, we were all connected by our concern for the Riveras. We included not only family and close friends, but friends of friends and people who, like I had, had been gifted with a heart for this specific story.

Next, I realized that the concept of #CONSTANT prayer couldn't be achieved by one person or even several people. The more people we had who were committed to praying, the more sustainable praying around the clock became.

These realizations led to two things for my to-do list. First, I needed to share the story of Dana with people who I knew would pray—thereby expanding my branch of the prayer team.

Next, I needed to find a way to introduce the Riveras to the people who were actively praying for them. How powerful would it be if they began to understand, even if only nominally, the number of strangers who had been called by God's love to do so?

In one of the many notebooks I kept on my desk, I sketched an idea: a Praying for You Profile. It would be like a baseball card or a hard copy of a Facebook profile. On the front it would have an actual photo of the person, plus a basic biographical sketch—including where they lived, their hometown, their connection to me, their alma mater, their job—and then a small paragraph called "the 411" with more personal information.

The real kicker was for the back of the card. This would be a game changer. Here, I planned on soliciting a message from the pray-er to the pray-ee. In other words, I would ask my people to write a few lines directly to the Riveras. In a stroke of creative genius, I would call this "message to you."

As a noncrafty person, I decided I would use my vintage typewriter and type the details on a large notecard. If I had known then how many Praying for You Profiles (PFYPs) I would eventually make, I would have come up with something more visually pleasing. These weren't ever, and I mean ever, going to be Etsy-worthy. No surprise there.

The first card I did—or PFYP #1—featured my dear friend and fellow sports lover Kristi Lamb, whom I had met in Ohio. She already knew the story of Dana, so I sent her a text asking her to help me out.

September 27, 2015, 1:10 p.m.

Hi! I'm working on something to introduce my friend Dana (the one I write weekly) to the people who are praying for her. You are up first. I would like to include a personal message from you on the bio, just a few words if you are willing. What do you think? #thanks

She obviously had a few questions, but, like virtually everyone I asked, she replied with a series of heartfelt words that had to have been inspired by God.

PFYP #1

Name: Kristi Lamb

Resides in: Centerville, Ohio

Hometown: Flint, Michigan

Connection: An Ohio BFF; our husbands work together

Alma mater: Michigan State

Job: Mom, professional grade

The 411: Other than me [Amy], the biggest female sports fan ever. Michigan State basketball and football fanatic. The Spartans, like LSU fans, love to hate on Nick Saban, who left them suddenly after five seasons when he took the LSU job. Kristi has a son who is a sophomore at Michigan State and two daughters, fifth and eighth grades.

Message to you: I am praying for peace for you. Although this is not something I have lived through personally, my husband lost his older brother, who was eighteen when my husband was fourteen. I have heard the stories of extreme sadness that only someone who has lived through such a tragedy can understand. I will be praying that each day God will comfort you with a small gift of happiness: a hug from a friend or family member, a smile from a stranger, a song on the radio, a beautiful blue sky. I pray that a little light shines on you each day to soften the darkness you are feeling.

Kristi Lamb

#CONSTANT

Though I've never saved a copy of anything else I've sent to Dana (except for her Facebook letter), I have kept copies of the PFYPs. Looking back over PFYP #1, I'm almost embarrassed by how many typos there were in the original version. These—which I fixed by hand—are all attributable to me, a crappy typist utilizing a vintage machine with no correction tape.

I also felt the need to add a splash of color by using my three highlighters (yellow, pink, and orange), which I typically used while looking at college football statistics, to highlight each of the categories on the card. Again, Etsy wasn't going to be a part of this situation.

I included PFYP #1 in Dana's weekly letter sometime in October 2015. I told her that I had clearly lost my mind again, explained the thinking behind the card, and then promised I'd send her a PFYP on a biweekly basis.

The PFYP project not only forced me to share the Riveras' story but gave me the opportunity to watch my friends, one by one, step up to the plate and send a heartfelt message to them. Every response humbled me, and I learned so much, both about how amazing my people are and about how big God's love is.

This side project also kicked off the Team #CONSTANT prayer team. Each person who participated in the PFYP initiative became an official member. Eventually the membership benefits included a small plastic card, the size of a credit card, featuring the Riveras' pictures, their names, and a reminder to pray for them daily. The group grew to approximately one hundred people and included people who weren't featured on a PFYP.

I realize now that the PFYP program was fueled by Dana's Facebook posts about National Childhood Cancer Awareness Month. Her posts on social media were doubling my efforts to go "old school."

∽ₑᴐ

I received another letter from Dana just after Thanksgiving. In it, she commented, for the first time, on the PFYPs.

Though visiting with God is challenging, it does amaze me how He continuously provides people like you and #CONSTANT warriors to cover us in prayer. The PFY Profiles are unreal! I cannot begin to tell you what they mean! #humbled! Thank you and yours!

This specific remark would likely have been important to anyone who had gotten so deeply invested in someone else's situation. Though it would have been counterintuitive to think the PFYPs were offensive, I did continually worry about being "over the top" in how I was handling my in-writing relationship with Dana. Did she really want or need a weekly discourse about my life? And how over the top did she think it was that I was sharing her story with strangers and asking them to get involved?

Her validation clearly wasn't necessary for me to continue being utterly ridiculous, but it certainly did spur me on to do even more—most of all, to pray continuously.

I will close with this: I am thankful that God chose you to minister to me! Love you! Dana

Letter #69

⚸

Letter #69 was to the mother of a student I had worked with during my time with the youth ministry at church. Though I didn't know her well and had interacted with her only on a handful of occasions, I had a strong sense that I liked her, first, because I had gotten a good impression of her during our brief personal encounters, and second, because her Facebook posts always made me suspect that we had a similar sense of humor and approach to life.

But that didn't mean that writing her a letter wasn't going to be awkward. While it's one thing to assume all sorts of things in your own head, it's entirely different to pontificate on those things in writing for two pages.

This explains why #66 was one of the very few recipients whom I didn't Facebook-message for an address and whom I instead resorted to stalking online. I felt truly ridiculous reaching out to her with a letter, especially because, since she lived locally and we attended the same church, I might have to see her in the flesh in the future.

December 4, 2015

One of the real upsides of this "project" thus far has been the opportunity to treat FB friends as actual individuals, as opposed to blips on my news feed. In other words, if you're going to try to write someone a letter, in horrible handwriting, then you need to learn more about them.

Yes, I stalked your page, and here's what I learned.

You grew up in Lincoln, Illinois, the only town to be

named for the president, before he was, well, the president.

I had no idea that you were from there. Are your people still there? Do you go back?

The other part that struck me is how supportive you are of your two daughters—a fact that has always shined through Katie, whom I so enjoyed getting to know in the youth ministry at church.

Please also know how much I personally enjoy your posts —especially the ones that expose your sense of humor. Those always make me think we would have a good time hanging out!

I can remember exactly where I was when I received #69's Facebook message. Willie and I were in Toronto for his office Christmas party, and we were both getting ready when my phone dinged. My reaction was a combination of laughter and awe. It was as if I'd already had my first two drinks, only the party hadn't even started yet. Or maybe it had.

December 11, 2015

Dear Facebook and real-life friend, I was very surprised and happy to receive your letter. It made my day ☺. I will be writing back once I finish my Christmas shopping ☺.

Sincerely,
Your Facebook and real-life friend

Then, even though #69 had promised in her electronic message that she would write back, I was thoroughly shocked and delighted all over again when I received a letter from her. It was six full pages about her background, from where she grew up to each member of her family to her kids and her job. It was everything that social media wasn't, and since I hadn't known much about #69 previously, it was everything I dreamed the letter-writing campaign could be.

It was as if Facebook didn't exist and we were friends writing in earnest about our lives. It was one of the greatest single outcomes of the project, and the fact that it was totally unexpected is no coincidence.

January 20, 2016

I can't tell you how much I enjoyed your letter. It was a surprise I never saw coming, and it really made my day. It's so rare to get a real letter with real handwriting.

She also made an addition to people's ever-expanding list of astute observations about social media.

I love how Facebook allows you to stay in touch with people who don't live close to you (or even ones who do) or reconnect with old friends, but I hate how it undermines the self-confidence of people, young and old, and causes them to live in a world of self-comparison. . . .

Best of all, #69 provided one of the greatest "lists" in the annals of pen-palling.

Yes, I am from Lincoln, Illinois, which, as you probably learned from your stalking/research, is located in the middle of many acres of corn and soybean fields. Here are some fun facts about my childhood there:

- *School colors were based on holidays. Halloween*

(orange and black) for junior high. Christmas (red and green) for high school.

- *Our high school mascot was a Railsplitter, which was basically Abraham Lincoln on steroids. The local beekeeper (yes, there was a local beekeeper) bore an uncanny resemblance to him, and once or twice every year he would do a log-splitting demonstration as the halftime show at high school basketball games.*
- *Grade-school field trips were always to New Salem, where Abraham Lincoln lived prior to becoming famous, but I was sick every time they went and never actually visited there until after my kids were born.*
- *I grew up on Grand Avenue, which was part of the GOP trilogy of streets in Lincoln (Grand, Ogelsby, and Palmer). Take a guess as to what the predominant political party was ☺.*
- *We lived one house (and an empty lot) away from Route 66, back when there weren't any interstates in Illinois and Route 66 was a heavily traveled highway.*

Letter #69 illustrated another common theme in the Facebook project: The people you think are least likely to reply are precisely the people you'll hear back from. And sometimes it's one of these folks, instead of the ones whom we expect to reply, who responds in a way that fills us with hope.

Letter #84

Letter #84 is an example of how you can be friends on social media without ever crossing paths physically. Number 84 and I had a mutual friend in real life: my camp friend Karen, whom I'd known since childhood. She and #84 did life together in their corner of the world.

Number 84 and I also shared a name. My maiden name, Weinland, was the same as her married name. Given what an unusual name it is, she friended me to learn more about our connection.

January 2, 2016

You and I are an interesting, unique scenario in this little project because we are friends because of FB. We met online but have never met in person, despite the fact that we have three mutual friends. I'd love to unlock the link between our families. Given the rarity of the name, it's likely our kids are actually blood related, even if only as far-off cousins. I may look into that and get back to you!

Overall, please know that I value our virtual friendship and appreciate the uniqueness of our friend status! Also, actual human beings look at your posts and pictures and enjoy both!

Because my connection with #84 was based entirely on social media, her handwritten reply, which I received within a couple of weeks of sending my letter, was yet another surprise.

January 20, 2016

First of all, I want to say thank you for the handwritten letter. So rare today to actually receive mail you actually enjoy! I did see your name as Karen's friend on FB and thought, "Wow, we must be related!" Sharing the Weinland name is very exciting—as I rarely meet anyone other than my husband's family with that name.

Thank you again for reaching out. "Real" is good in the cyber-world we live in.

Love, #84

Number 84's reply was part of a large stack of mail that came that day. After reading her letter, I went back through the mail and found an envelope addressed to "Amy Weinland," which was peculiar for its lack of my married name.

I saw that the return address was from a benefits company in Shreveport, Louisiana, the same town where #84 resided.

Opening it with intrigue, I received my second surprise of the day—it was a letter from #84's husband, who had written me separately the same day she had! In it, he thanked me for my letter to his wife and then began by stating, "With a note to the obvious, I am the Weinland of the family, so I will begin the discourse."

I connected with the tone of his letter immediately and found an odd familiarity in his prose. "We are located in Louisiana only because the twisting road of life brought me here. Met a girl, and here I stayed. A story familiar to many a man." Not only were his words well put together, but he sprinkled in dashes of humor: "We have a middle-school daughter somewhere in the house, but she is elusive these days."

He went on to inquire about our branch of the Weinland

family, explained his own ancestry, and then even generously offered to share an extensive Weinland genealogy report his aunt had compiled.

He closed with a story about our shared name.

There is a folksy band called Weinland from Oregon. I met the band members when they were on tour in the South. It was interesting to watch the lead singer's face when I gave him my business card. Apparently, his mother was a Weinland and he took that name as a middle name.

So that is the essence of it. Happy to continue this interesting conversation among us, the rare breed that is Weinland.

This was the only time I'd receive a reply to a letter from someone other than the recipient. It was also a relationship that would continue—at least in writing and electronically—beyond the Facebook project and into the future. It is my hope that one day we'll meet in person and rejoin our distant branches of the same family tree. What would our Weinland ancestors think about our reconnecting via something as futuristic as the internet?

For all social media's concrete flaws, it had connected my family and me with people who were likely blood relatives who we didn't even know existed. All this from a "friend of a friend" whom I'd never even spoken to on the phone, much less met in person. This situation underscores an upside of the digital age: the opportunity to find and then connect in a meaningful way with people who otherwise would be totally unknown to us.

Letter #90

᳘

Letter #90 was to a guy I had met at camp. He was from a family with several siblings who were members of the same subset of campers and counselors that I had attended Olympia with. While I wasn't close with him or any of his people, we had grown up during the same era at camp. That meant that we shared the same memories, were connected to the same people, and were influenced by the same unique culture. It was a lot like being cousins.

January 8, 2016

The good news is, despite the fact that it's been quite some time since we saw each other in person, we are part of the same camp family, so this, writing you, is decidedly less awkward than the dreaded "Hi, do you remember me from seventh-grade band—you played the flute, and I was a big dork?" letter. Trust me, I've written that letter.

One of the real upsides of this project has been the opportunity to treat FB friends as actual individuals, as opposed to blips on my news feed. Some would call it stalking, but I call it digging deeper. In your case, I found out that you are expecting a baby! By the look of things, the arrival ought to be very close. Congrats on that, friend, and know I'll say a prayer for your little family.

More than anything, please know that I value our camp connection, our family ties, and your friendship. I care about you and your people and what happens in your life. It's all stuff that simply cannot be quantified by "likes" or comments.

Though I told #90 that I didn't experience any awkwardness while writing him, that's not entirely true. The fact that #90 is male was a jumping-off point for my hesitancy. Somehow, I assumed that the readers of my letters who had penises would welcome my words with less exuberance than those who were otherwise equipped. My thinking was that the letters, and sharing, would resonate more on an emotional level with women than with men.

My assumption regarding gender, combined with the fact that I had never been personally close with #90—while we were certainly more than mere acquaintances, we also weren't full-fledged friends—resulted in self-doubt. This uncertainty—which I experienced repeatedly to varying degrees while writing the letters—led to a lack of conviction about the entire project. It was exhausting.

It also meant that in no way did I expect a response from #90. But, once again, that's precisely what happened, this time via Facebook Messenger.

February 18, 2016

Amy, I got your letter, and I have to say that you undertook quite a project! It's true when you say that we sometimes treat these people with whom we had past relationships like blips on a news feed. And I'm glad you reached out and made me human again.

Because of the time I've been spending with our new baby, and since my handwriting is much worse than yours, I'll have to respond on FB this time.
It's nice when someone goes out of their way to reach out to an old friend—I appreciate it, and I'm sure everyone you wrote letters did too.

So, you talked about real life . . . I'm getting a big dose of that right now. My wife and I have had a pretty adventurous relationship, living abroad, traveling to fifty-plus countries, flying for a living, sailing, scuba diving, etc. Basically, doing the unusual. And now we have this little person who completely relies on us to learn, to survive, to be shown the world . . . Crazy. So now we're figuring out how to keep our lifestyle but fully include our new baby girl. Because our best gift to her (we feel) is to show her the world and how it works, how other people live, so at least she has the tools to be tolerant and understanding of others and their culture. Such a big task! Thanks for reaching out. It's good to know that real people are behind the veil of FB.

While from a purely logical standpoint we are continuously aware that real people living very real lives are behind each profile on Facebook, that's easy to forget emotionally. Our inability to see, touch, and personally witness the people we're connected to on social media can cause us to relegate them to prefabricated molds consisting exclusively of what we've seen via their comments, photos, shares, and likes.

The simple and seemingly ordinary act of writing someone a letter has the magical power to transform individuals from electronic creatures to flesh-and-bone, living, breathing, imperfect yet marvelous human beings.

Letter #100

❧

Letter #100 marked a major milestone in the project. I had written 100 letters in 181 days, for an average of half a letter per day. Though well short of the lofty goal of 1.4 letters per day I'd laid out at the beginning of the project, I had made it way beyond the starting point. I felt physically different. A buzz of energy vibrated throughout me, resulting in a sense that I was moving in the right direction. It was a lot like that feeling you get after the first month of a new exercise-and-diet regime. Though you aren't transformed yet and the scale doesn't say what you thought it would, you feel different in the same pants you've been wearing for the past couple of years.

The recipient of letter #100 was a guy whom I had worked with during my time as a purchasing agent in the adult-beverage industry.

January 17, 2016

Dear #100,

Greetings—or, as Adele once said, "Hello from the other side!" So, first things first: Why in the world am I writing you an actual letter, on paper, with a pen? That's a great question. Recently, I've been wondering what being friends on Facebook is all about. What does it even mean? It all started when I wanted to send a FB friend a few supportive cards as her son was battling cancer. My plan was flawless—that is, until I realized that not only had I not spoken to this person in thirty-plus years (weird, because I'm only thirty-seven), but I had no clue what her address was, because, well, you know, we're "just FB friends."

That got me thinking: What's the difference between "real" people and "just FB" ones? Or, instead, are they all the same—actual individuals with actual cares and concerns—only I have come to approach them differently? I mean, sure, I "know" all these people, or at least I knew them—but is this really being in relationship? Then I got a ridiculous idea: What would happen if I tried to write each and every one of my FB people a letter. Would I even have anything to say? Would it be the most awkward thing ever?

That all brings me here—to your letter. So, we haven't seen each other since our mutual days at Republic Beverage, or was it Julius Schepps then? Regardless, that did not deter me from being very excited when I drew your name out of my box of people to write to (yes—this is clearly a project that honors the scientific method). The reason for my excitement was twofold: 1) I remember you very fondly from our beverage days and have always, even before we reconnected on FB, counted you as one of the high points in terms of quality people I connected with during that time period. And when I say "quality," I include your whole Longhorn affiliation, appreciating not so much your burnt-orange attire, but your passion for your school and team. And 2) I truly enjoy and delight in "keeping up" with you and your family on FB—loving the window into your West Coast world.

That said, I have questions—for instance, where did you meet Mrs. #100? What took you to LA? I'm assuming your job, but maybe not? I count what look like three beast soccer playing kids—is that correct? How old are they? What grades in school are they? What are their other interests?

As for me, we've been in the Dayton, Ohio, area (forty-five minutes north of Cincinnati) since 2007. Other than the weather, it's a lot like LA. . . . Okay, well, it's not. Other than the inflated value, given Big 10 football, it's a great place to live. We have two kids: Will (eighteen, a senior in high school) and Matthew (nine, in fourth grade). Will is looking to attend either Ohio University (photography and design) or University of Cincinnati (industrial design) in the fall. I stay home and freelance write. All in all, it's amazing, tragic, thrilling, boring, joyous, and unsettling. In other words, it's real life!

More than anything, I want you to know that I value our past connection and your friendship on Facebook and in real life. I enjoy your photos and well-thought-out posts and care about you, your family, and what is happening in your life. It's all stuff that simply cannot be quantified in "likes" or comments.

Take care and all the best,

Amy W. D.

Your friend in REAL life

#iamaredraider #donthate #congratulate

Number 100 responded with a handwritten, two-page letter. I received it in my mailbox less than two weeks after I wrote him. Given that he was on the West Coast and I was in the Midwest, he must have written me back immediately and then made the effort to put his response in the mail just as quickly.

January 30, 2016

Dear Amy,

What a pleasant surprise to read your letter. It's been way too long. My wife and I moved to Los Angeles in 2003. I took a supplier job with a winery when they offered to pay for my move. Since I moved here, I have stayed working in the industry with a few companies. We have made lots of new friends and love it here. Our family does most of our activities in Santa Monica, so we enjoy great weather 95 percent of the time.

Our three kids keep our weekends very busy with sports games and tournaments. All three play soccer year-round now. They love it and do other stuff beyond school too. My daughter can really sing well, so she has lots of rehearsals with her choir and musical theater group.

I'm glad to read that you are enjoying Ohio and football fans. I have a close friend who drives me a little crazy with his "OSU is great" FB posts every week. Plenty of good people in the Midwest, though.

Great to catch up the old-fashioned way, by written letter. I'm explaining this to my seven-year-old right now. I'll keep enjoying your wit and humor on FB—so post often and post funny.

Hugs,

#100

While not dripping with meaning or full of life lessons, my exchange with #100 demonstrated perfectly what the Facebook project was all about. It was hundreds of private, one-on-one conversations—conducted via old-school letters and electronically—between two *friends*. While "catching up" and then sharing memories, thoughts, ideas, and love may seem like nothing more than a normal function of human relations, in the culture of social media—which has a way of sucking the individuality out of each of us—it is extraordinary.

January 2016

I had decided not to tell Dana about the Facebook project until I had reached the point where I felt like it was "for real" and sustainable. In other words, I didn't want to tell her that she'd inspired me to behave irrationally until I was sure I could follow through on the promise.

The one hundred–letter mark seemed like an appropriate time to share. It was also January 2016, the first anniversary of Parker's death. Though I didn't plan the timing and was sure it would have no bearing on the very real pain and suffering Dana was experiencing, I suppose I hoped that telling her would serve as some sort of underwhelming diversion. Perhaps that's what I was hoping all my in-writing communication to her would be.

"The Facebook project is the result of God's love for you and your family, the same love that was somehow inserted into my own human heart and inspired me to write to you and pray for your family," I told her. "This love oozed over into the idea to write everyone a letter." I continued, "If my experience with you —somebody I hadn't seen or spoken to in thirty years, and whose address I didn't even know—was so life-changing, what was out there behind the other five hundred names listed on my Facebook profile?"

I went so far as to tell her that it was "our" project, even though she had never had the opportunity to confirm her participation. I finished by using the hashtags that I eventually copied into my journal. #godslove #soreal #icantshutup.

It was as true as anything I'd ever said to her.

Updating Dana after I'd written the next one hundred Facebook letters became another one of the standard practices of the project. It was something I looked forward to—hitting two hundred, three hundred, four hundred, and finally five hundred—so I could update her on how "our" endeavor was coming along.

She never commented on the project in writing, but eventually, one by one, each of her four daughters—Mady and Peyton, and then Alli and Lauren—friended me on Facebook. It meant that ultimately my two letter-writing campaigns were destined to intersect.

Right around the same time I wrote letter #100, I received another letter from Dana. She had written it in pieces from late November through the first half of December.

She started by commenting on a series of pictures I had sent her of our kitchen, which we had gutted and were redoing. I had included the photos as yet another attempt to fill pages and envelopes. What I didn't know, and couldn't have known, was that this topic—home improvement—was one of her absolute passions. It became a major thread in our future letters and conversations.

Amy:

So, FIRST! I am addicted to home renovation, decorating, HGTV . . . so I am waiting anxiously for the pics of your kitchen! I would love to flip houses, but the market in Laffy is not right for that. We renovated our last two homes and begin renos on this one in a week or

so. Really, most of the work is outside, though we are
raising a few doorways and putting French doors where
some windows are. I will attempt to send pics; I usually
forget to take the "before" photos! Thanks for including
me in the kitchen redo!

She also made some observations on what the holidays look like for those who are grieving.

Thanksgiving week was much harder than I anticipated.
Peyton was out of town until Wednesday, so I was alone
more than usual. Alli came over lots during the day
because we were both off for the week, and that helped.
I've never been a loner and know that's why God gave me
five kids. Jim's nephew and wife came in from Atlanta,
my brother from Alabama, and we had a full house from
Wednesday to today!! Literally FULL! That helped, but
waking up with an aching heart daily is just rough!

Finally, she included details of her family's trip to Memphis in early December to participate in the St. Jude Marathon weekend. Though she didn't tell me this directly, I had read via her fundraising campaign for the race that she had originally signed up to participate while Parker was still with them. Her intention was to use it as a way to celebrate the end of Parker's second treatment plan. Instead, now she was running, and raising money, to honor his life.

So, as you can see on Facebook, we were surrounded by
nothing but pure LOVE! We had a magical time,
actually. We took Memphis by storm! The good news is,

EVERYONE who went asked to go back next year, so we will do it again. We won't raise as much money, because I'm tired, but we will do the race. Think about joining us —first weekend in December. There's a 5k, a half, and even a relay ☺.

Although I didn't know it at the time, that final sentence planted another important seed.

Letter #126

Letter #126 was to a childhood friend whom I went all the way through high school with. Though I'm sure we saw each other as we got older, the bulk of our actual time together came when we were younger, playing soccer together and living in the same neighborhood. She was another case of someone whom I had not spoken to in thirty years.

The letter itself contained shades of the other lessons I had learned one hundred letters into the project. As the process continued, I found myself using little bits and pieces of friends' observations in my own.

February 16, 2016

So, first, the obvious question: Why in the world am I writing you an actual letter? Well, recently I've been wondering what being "friends" on Facebook is all about. My pondering began in earnest when I wanted to send a FB friend a condolence card, and then a series of notes, as her son had tragically died after battling cancer. My plan was flawless—that is, until I realized that not only had I not actually spoken to this person in thirty-plus years, but I had no clue what her address was, because, well, you know, we're "just FB" friends. That got me thinking: What's the difference between "real" people and "just FB" ones? Or, instead, are they all the same—actual individuals with actual cares and concerns—only I've begun approaching them differently in my own head and heart? Then I took a big, irrational leap forward and wondered what would happen if I tried to write all of my

FB people a letter. Could it help me to move all of my friends back into the same group?

I suppose the upside of FB is, as shallow and almost scary as it is, at least we have some feel for what happened next. You and I both have an idea of what happened to each other "next."

The recipient of #126 replied via her own letter four months after I wrote her. Beyond providing a sweeping review of her life from 1986 to 2016, her reply reflected two common ongoing themes associated with the project. The first was the almost unbelievable timing of my letter, which in her case coincided with when she found out about our mutual friend Nicole's suicide.

June 14, 2016

Your letter had such uncanny timing to it. Following the news of Nicole taking her own life, I wonder about FB friends as well. I have to admit, reading your letter had me in tears—both sad and happy. I heard the news of Nicole in the middle of the Super Bowl, just six days before you wrote to me.

Next, she made a keen observation about social media by sharing a personal story.

I do have a couple of people I consider truly Facebook friends.... I met a coworker's wife at a Christmas party three years ago. She was really fun, and we hit it off great. She friended me the next day. I have yet to see her again but know she has a baby and that they were camping this weekend. I am not friends with her husband, and we actually don't work in the same group, so I only work with him every so often, and sometimes I think, "I know way more about him and his life than he does about mine," which is a bit awkward. So, since then, I have been trying to limit my Facebook friends to people I know, rather than people I have just met briefly. For me, it is staying connected and not necessarily a way to connect, if that makes sense.

Though we can stay apprised of some of the highlights of a Facebook friend's life—at least the parts they are willing to share—that does not provide an actual link between us and that person. There's a big difference between looking in from the outside and actually being on the inside of somebody's life.

Letter #137

Letter #137 was to my only aunt, my dad's sister. It was significant on several levels, the first of which is that our family, like countless others, isn't proficient at sharing feelings. So, while I have years and years of history with my aunt, we've never spoken of it. I always considered that a good thing.

However, when I wrote my aunt, we had recently had what for me had been a transformative conversation. She and my uncle had visited us in Ohio, and I had asked her questions about my past. It blossomed into one of the most meaningful, honest discussions I'd ever had, one that put into perspective and validated much of my emotional foundation. The letter was my opportunity to say thank you on both levels.

February 27, 2016

One of the real upsides of writing these letters (you are #137) has been the opportunity to say things to key people in my life. In some instances, I didn't even know how much I had to say until I got going. I have also learned, along the way, that there is a certain freeing element in the lost art of letter writing. I think knowing that you won't get an immediate response and knowing that by the time the other person receives it, you'll already have forgotten parts of it gives you a certain freedom to say more and speak more openly.

To you, my only aunt, I've always wanted to say thanks. When I think of you, I think not only of the close tie we've created during my marriage to Willie—you two taking the time to visit us in England and Ohio, plus our golf outings—but also of the impact and positive influence you had on me as a kid.

You always encouraged me and took time to talk to me. I get that that kind of thing might not seem like a huge deal, but now that I'm older and have two kids and nine nieces and nephews, I understand the effort that it took on your part. Also, as someone who has struggled with self-confidence, I now realize that your regular, positive influence is a huge, very real part of my making it to 2016 as a whole, happy individual. And then there was our most recent conversation, during your last visit here. Your honesty and, again, your positive remarks during that time were nothing short of life-changing. Amazingly, it was one of the most honest conversations I've ever had about my early life.

While my aunt did not respond in writing, she did mention the letter when I saw her at my father-in-law's memorial service in Houston at the beginning of March. That would have been just days after she received the letter. In classic Weinland family form, we didn't discuss the content of the letter. Instead, we laughed about the scope and the absurd nature of the project itself.

What I did feel was a difference when she hugged me. Or perhaps that was just me feeling closer to her because I had shared the love I have for her, not out loud, but on paper, where we could both keep it forever.

While it's generally accepted that telling somebody that you love, value, and appreciate them is about making *them* feel good, perhaps the person who walks away the most changed is you.

Letter #155

Letter #155 was a classic example of what you might say in a random note to a friend of a friend. Number 155 and her family have a long-term close relationship with my brother and sister-in-law. That meant I usually saw them at least once a year, often at our family place in Texas.

Though this relationship wasn't necessarily "mine," it was one I was active in, so the letter gave me an opportunity to express thanks and point out similarities in our lives.

March 18, 2016

I want you to know how much I enjoy being around you —that is, when I get lucky enough to be in Texas and in the same place as you and your people. You have such a great energy and have always made me feel welcome and 100 percent a part of whatever is going on. That's a big deal, and much appreciated by someone who is not a part of your group but loves being a visitor.

I also wanted to say that I will be praying for you and your daughter as she goes away to college in the fall. And I humbly ask for your prayers as our Will sets off for Ohio University this fall. We are lucky to be going through this at the same time—count on my support from afar.

I received a reply from #155 just over a week after I wrote to her. It came via Facebook Messenger and included a picture, which wasn't unusual, as a handful of recipients who responded electronically included a photo of my letter after they had opened it. What set #155's reply apart was that attached to it was a selfie depicting her reaction to the letter. She was apparently in her bathroom, with tears streaming down her face.

March 26, 2016

Just got your lovely real-life letter, and can I just say, I am blown away. I can't tell you how timely it was and how appreciative I am for you and your thoughtfulness! I'm going to write you a real letter back. I want to follow your example. I just couldn't forgo telling you immediately THANK YOU for your kind and heartfelt words.

My initial reaction to the photo was to laugh. Her sharing, though clearly sincere, had a comical element to it, I think because she responded in a way that I wouldn't or couldn't have.

After I had time to reflect, I realized that the picture had everything to do with how much the letter had meant to her. She responded to things that made her feel something deeply in a very authentic, vulnerable way.

If I wanted the recipients of my letters to accept me—as the sender and the sharer of feelings—right where I was, that was exactly the approach I should take with the respondents. It wasn't just about not getting caught up in who did and didn't reply; I needed to allow people to acknowledge my words in their own unique way, and celebrate each one of them for doing so.

One-on-one communication is unpredictable. When we're allowed to participate in dialogue in a free space—where we feel completely at liberty to be ourselves—everybody, on both sides of the equation, is changed.

Letter #169

Letter #169 was to the mom of one of my close friends in Ohio, Michelle. She and I were both members of a group of families who had relocated from Texas to the Dayton area. The core group consisted of five couples and a variety of kids, who were also friends. We operated like a family. Physically separated from our biological people, we relied on each other for everything from what to do at Easter to whom to call in the middle of the night. The best illustration of what we meant to one another was that we were all listed as each other's emergency contacts on school, sports, and medical forms.

The recipient of letter #169 lived in Texas but spent a lot of her time in Ohio, visiting Michelle's family. She and her husband were part of "us."

Number 169 is special, one of those people who don't fit into a single generation but instead just blend in with and thrive among any age group. She is a great encourager, especially for women and moms, always willing to lend advice and add perspective. She even babysat for kids who weren't her grandchildren and provided an experience that most of our kids missed because of our geographic dislocation.

She is one of those rare people who insert themselves delicately into your business. You don't even know she's there until you need her, and she has the gift of knowing when to retreat.

March 31, 2016

One of the best parts of this "experiment" thus far has been the opportunity to express myself to so many amazing people. It's stuff that otherwise would likely have gone unsaid. (Also, I've discovered that noninstantaneous communication is both freeing and powerful.)

To you: 1) I hope you know the high regard that we all hold you in—and that applies to me especially. Your openness, genuine warmth, and willingness to get involved in our lives is very special. You make everybody feel so accepted and listened to. Honestly, although I'm personally sort of a closed book, I feel like I could tell you anything and would be better for it.

2) You are super intelligent and wise. Having you as a friend (not just as "my friend's mom") is incredibly humbling—like, what is this amazing woman being my friend for? I think it's safe to say you make both my real-life friends list and my Facebook friends list more legit.

3) Thank you for being invested in our kids' lives— especially mine. You are a special gift to our children. It's something that can actually be gauged, in terms of impact, by the genuine LOVE they have for you. My kids are better for knowing you. Thanks a million times over for caring about them.

In closing, there is a lot of cheese here, so it's probably best that we never speak of it. That of course does not mean that I am not sincere—because I mean everything I've said and I love you even though your husband is a Texas A&M Aggie!

Given my high regard for #169, I wasn't surprised that she responded and that she did so in a way that made me look at what I was doing from a different angle.

May 8, 2016

Dear Amy,

My first thought when I saw your letter was actually, "I am so excited because there is something handwritten for ME!" I am a huge fan of handwritten ANYTHING.

Within the last couple of months, I have brought out my saved letters and lost myself not only in the words they contain but also in the handwriting of the people I have loved. I despaired of the thought that my grandkids could come across something and not realize that it was my handwriting, or Grandpa's handwriting, or, worse yet, their own parents'! It is something I don't want to slip through our fingers—personal thoughts, feelings, anecdotes assigned to keyboards break my heart.

The fact that I'm not sure how to refer to #169—is she my friend, or my friend's mom, or a mentor, or a quasi-aunt?—reminds us that relationships don't need preestablished labels to exert tremendous influence. Someone can make meaningful contributions to our lives even if we can't define who they are to us or how they fit in. It's something that is true even if that person isn't a regular visitor in our daily life.

The recipient of letter #169 reminds us there are lessons to be learned from these people that while, perhaps not obvious (like their places in our own lives), have the potential to be profound.

March 2016

*E*arly that spring, I received another letter from Dana. Her first order of business was to thank me for praying for her granddaughter, who also happened to be named Amy.

Her gratitude referred to a prayer request she had sent me via Facebook Messenger. Little Amy—the daughter of Jim and Dana's oldest daughter, Alli—was in the hospital with a virus. It marked the first time Dana had ever contacted me electronically and the first time she had sent a real-time prayer request.

> Please constant for Baby Amy. She has a virus in her lil' lungs and is in the hospital. Doing better than last night when she got there, but still . . . I may not check Facebook a lot, so, just for future reference, here's my cell number. Love you, pal.

Not only did this give me an opportunity to pray for something Rivera-related instantaneously, but the exchange of our cell numbers (I responded with mine) marked another milestone in what was otherwise an in-writing-only relationship. I also loved how Dana used "constant" as a verb—as if it were a verifiable service.

In the remainder of the letter, she went deep about where they were with their overwhelming grief and how they had spent the first anniversary of Parker's passing.

*New Year's, which I anticipated being awful, was okay.
We went to the beach with four other families from the
26th to the 2nd. All my kids came, as well as my nieces
and others, so we were surrounded by loved ones. It just
doesn't get easier, nor do I want it to. Waking up daily
with a heavy heart is just how we live. We aren't good—
we will never be good—but what we ARE is covered in
prayer! I know this to be true—#CONSTANT and so
many others pray for us daily, and I know that is what
gets us up and going. We are also trying to live like Parker
—with faith and acceptance. It is hard, but there are
really peaceful moments in knowing he is with Jesus. The
impact he made still blows my mind as people continue to
tell us stories about his impact.*

*I myself think A LOT about ALL the suffering. There was
SO much, and I witnessed every bit of it. He NEVER
ONCE said, "This sucks" or, "Why Me?" Instead, he
would bite on a rag (because the pain was so bad) and
tell me he was sorry. He always apologized for everything
—throwing up, incontinence, needing things . . .
ALWAYS. Of course I said, "Parker—PLEASE!!! Don't
apologize." But he hated seeing me watch him suffer. For
that I am grateful—the suffering is over, and he is pain
free in heaven.*

No matter how much time passes, these words will always
make me feel physically ill—nauseated and unable to breathe
regularly.

Though I'll never be able to pinpoint why Dana shared in
such a deep way, I have come to believe it's a combination of our
incredible connection and the freedom of noninstantaneous
communication.

I wasn't supposed to be in her life in 2016. As tenuous as the link between us was, it was equally powerful. I believe it impacted both of us deeply long before it ever registered with us cognitively.

Then there was the fact that, for the first couple of years after our reconnection, we communicated exclusively in writing. Our deep thoughts, updates, and feelings crossed in the mail. This meant we had no way to respond in real time. The overlapping created even a bigger sense of freedom. I believe we both shared more liberally because we had a chance to lose track of what we'd said. We also had zero expectations about when our messages would be received or responded to.

The blueprint of noninstantaneous communication also meant that I didn't feel pressure to respond immediately—if ever—to the deep things Dana shared. This was a very good thing, because there were obviously no words I could offer her that would ever be adequate.

What resulted was the realization that sometimes we're not going to have the right words to say, because they don't exist. What we do have, instead of a well-meaning and/or cliché phrase, is the opportunity to simply be there for another person.

Being present, available, or involved, not just in a physical sense, is as important as or more important than having words that are impossible to find in the first place.

Sometimes silence—combined with presence—is the best support.

Letter #173

Number 173 was another friend I had met through Olympia. Though I'm not sure we ever worked together, we both had solid roots at camp. She was also one of my Facebook friends who looked to have an almost perfect situation. Though I understood, especially given that I was 170 letters into my experiment when I wrote her, that Facebook told only part of the story, I was almost jealous of #173.

First, she was gorgeous—and I mean she is one of those fortysomethings who photograph like a model. Next, she was newly married to a successful and handsome professional who looked to be loaded. Then there was her lifestyle—pictures of her and her equally attractive friends sipping champagne while a professional photographer snapped magazine-worthy pictures of them on boats, at beaches, and sidled up to suave cocktail bars.

Yes, I was happy for her, but I found myself asking what is often the first question about social media: "What does her lifestyle say about my lifestyle?" It's embarrassing but true—but, seriously, what was I doing wrong? I mean, I could buy champagne, but where was I going to get a boat, or a swimsuit that didn't make me want to call my therapist? My life was very good, but hers appeared to be very better.

April 3, 2016

The great thing about camp connections is that the years and miles can separate us, but we always manage to reconnect immediately and pick back up just where we left off. And that's what's so great about Facebook. While, yes, it can be questionable, at least we get a window into each other's worlds.

And that brings me to my next point: I love following you on Facebook. In fact, I feel like I've lived through your wedding (gorgeous!) and so many other adventures with you. I also love seeing your son growing into quite the handsome young man. So while I may not always comment or hit "like," please know how much I enjoy seeing you and your beautiful smile online.

I hope your real life is full of more good than bad, and I hope love is always present.

Number 173's handwritten response, which I received just weeks after I wrote her, was a major turning point in the history of the project and to my approach to social media.

April 28, 2016

Dear Amy,

Your letter was timed perfectly. I received it the day after I was diagnosed with generalized anxiety disorder. I have always been an anxious person and sometimes sad on the inside but until now never really knew what the heck was wrong with me! So frustrating, right? But the worst part is that you can't really tell anyone that you have an anxiety disorder, or they think you belong in a loony bin! LOL. Now I have started to observe all of the people in my life, and it seems like the ones who I think have it all together are the most boring ☺. After all, life is hard enough. Without real people in my life that I can be open and honest with, I would be lost. So I am very happy that you have faith in real friendship! It restored my faith also!

Where I had seen #173's life—as depicted on Facebook—as a version of "perfect," even going so far as to assume it was superior to my own life, it wasn't. She was struggling, just like the rest of us, but in a different way. And, as if that weren't enough, she was grappling with something that she felt she couldn't share without being judged further.

And I was one of the people judging her life.

The other element that I found unsettling was what #173 said about friendship. I had, via my letter, restored her "faith in real friendship." She shared her diagnosis with me because she felt like I was a real friend, someone who cared.

And while I did care, truly, about #173, I knew I couldn't be there for her in real life like a legitimate, in-person friend needed to be.

It was one of the biggest takeaways of the Facebook project: I couldn't be there for all of my 580 Facebook friends, not because I didn't care, but because it was impossible.

That's why it's so important that we separate our social media relationships from those we do in "real life." Yes, we may feel connected to and care about our Facebook people, but we need to cultivate our in-person relationships, not only for our own well-being, but for the well-being of others.

I still feel guilty that I wasn't there, as a true friend, for #173. I did send her a telegram, and I know she knows that I care. But, sadly, that's the end of the story about our direct communication.

While I can't ever rectify that, I can be diligent about being present for the people in my small circle of friends. And if those in #173's group of intimates take similar action, drawing an invisible line between "real" and "virtual," then she will be cared for in the way she should be.

Letter #185

The recipient of Letter #185 and I have had two life intersections. First, our husbands worked together in Houston in the late 1990s and early 2000s, so we saw each other and chatted at a variety of company functions. Next, hers was one of the original families that moved—at the same time we did in 2007—from Texas to Ohio. Though her time there was far shorter than mine (she moved back to Houston after about five years in Dayton), we did get closer, especially early on.

> *April 14, 2016*
>
> *First things first: I was very excited to pull your name out of the box (yes—I'm very scientific) because I feel like we need to have a big catch-up. In other words, how are you? How is your family? How is Texas? I realize that a letter is a bit of a one-way communication, but at least it's something! Would love to hear what's going on with you.*
>
> *More than anything, I want you to know how much I value our long connection and your friendship. I do enjoy seeing you on Facebook and am thankful for the window it gives me into your world. Also, I have always admired all your talents (athletic and otherwise) and your commitment to your (our) faith. Many of your Facebook posts are inspirational—and that's the truth, regardless of how many "likes" or comments they may garner.*

Number 185 didn't respond until almost a year after I wrote her. By the time I received her handwritten response, I'd written an additional 357 Facebook letters. This lengthy lapse didn't diminish how deeply her reply resonated with me. I could physically feel her words; they were like a power surge.

March 23, 2017

Thank you so much for reaching out and writing. Your letter really touched my heart. I had been praying for someone to say hi because I was feeling very lonely at the time.

Hopes, wishes, and prayers can receive responses in the most random ways. In some magical cases, without any intention on our part, we get to play a role in the delivery of these answers.

For the most part, we can never know the positive effect we have on others, because only on rare occasions do we find out what happened after we played our part. Letter #185 is one of those atypical glimpses into the unseen, but completely real, process of impacting another person's life.

Letter #191

Letter #191 was to my sister-in-law on Willie's side of the family. Though not close in a BFF way, we are married to brothers and in twenty-five-plus years have done lots of life together. Most important, we share the same in-laws, which may be one of the most underrated connecting points in the history of human relations.

April 18, 2016

Of all the people God could have hooked me up with on the "other side" of the family, I'm glad and thankful it was you specifically. It's hard for a twentysomething to understand how significant these relationships are going to be—the family you marry into, and especially the people they marry, your natural allies in the world of in-laws. I'm very, very glad and blessed that it's specifically YOU that I'll sit next to at weddings, baby showers, and funerals. I got very lucky the day we got shoved into the bathroom together with our future mother-in-law yelling. Thank God that was you and not some yay-hoo!

While #191 didn't respond to my letter in writing, she did mention it when her and her family visited Ohio that May for Will's high school graduation. Not surprisingly, she mentioned it in a room filled with people and was crystal clear about how it made her feel.

"I cried when I read it," she said, "I didn't expect to, but I boo-hooed. I've never, ever received anything like that before. I'll save it forever."

It was as big a compliment as I or my little project would ever receive.

Letter #191 illustrates yet another common thread in the fabric of the project. Namely, if I hadn't been crazily writing letters, I would never have said what I said to my sister-in-law.

What's interesting in the case of #191 is that I had written a short couple of meaningful paragraphs about her and our relationship a few years earlier. I had always wanted to share those things with her but never had. The letter gave me the opportunity to do just that. I could never have known how emotionally satisfying it would be to pull the trigger on expressing myself to #191. It was yet another check mark on the to-do list I didn't even know I'd been keeping. We should never be afraid to go ahead and boldly say the things we've always wanted to say to another person.

Letter #200

Letter #200 meant several things—most critically that I had written 200 freaking letters, and in 288 days, no less. In case you were wondering, and I certainly was, that's 0.7 letters per day. I was almost in awe of myself.

Despite my exuberance, reaching this milestone was also daunting. Now I knew how hard it was to write two hundred letters. Now I knew that the callus on my right ring finger was going to grow bigger and hurt even more. Now I knew how exhausting it was going to be emotionally. Now I knew that despite what a life-changing experience it had already been, I was going to have to push myself through every single word. Now I knew what it meant that I had 380 letters remaining to write.

Yay for me, and also OMG!

The recipient of Letter #200 was a high school friend whom I hadn't seen since we embarked on the proverbial "rest of our lives."

April 28, 2016

This is letter #200 in my experiment, so it's also a bit of a milestone. That said, I guess there is no actual pomp and circumstance associated with this big moment, since I am in Ohio and you are in Texas and by the time you read this a week or so will have passed. But please know that if I could, I would present you with a ceremonial ham—or something like that.

Number 200 responded by posting on Facebook. Included with her words was a photo of the top of the letterhead and part of the envelope. This was always a double-edged sword, because where I delighted in my letter-writing campaign being recognized publicly, I worried that visibility would diminish its impact by compromising the element of surprise.

It also meant that other friends, when they found out what I was doing, would expect a letter from me. This thought fueled the growing pressure I felt to finish and therefore successfully reach out to each of my friends. But letter #200 was also proof that you truly can do anything you put your mind to.

May 2, 2016

Just got the most special letter from someone I haven't seen in the flesh in 30 years . . . . Such a treat! Love this and you, Amy Weinland Daughters! You have made me laugh for years and years. You have been the queen of random funnies since way before there was a Seinfeld!

May 2016

*D*ana's May letter was written on Easter Sunday. In it, she addressed the Praying for You Profiles, which were still going strong and which I inserted every other week into my letters to her.

> *The PFYPs AMAZE me! YOU AND YOURS AMAZE*
> *EVERY ONE OF US EACH AND EVERY WEEK! Jim*
> *said this morning how unbelievable it was that God put*
> *you in our path thirty years ago, knowing He would use*
> *you in our darkest days. The only way it makes sense is*
> *that God ordained it! You will NEVER, EVER KNOW*
> *WHAT YOU HAVE BECOME TO US!*

These words, and specifically those recounting what Jim had said, solidified both my continued efforts for the Rivera family and the Facebook project. If there had ever been any question about what I was supposed to do, this answered it.

Dana also shared a story about her BFF's sister losing a child.

> *You remember Heidi, my BFF since college. Well, two*
> *weeks ago, her sister's youngest (eighteen) child was killed*
> *in a car wreck! So it's been a rough time for us, and*

*grieving for her has added pain to my own process. I also
know what's in store for her, and my heart hurts for that.
That said, Heidi has stayed w/her (she's long divorced)
every night since. Heidi also came here every day until I
returned to work—the guard who lets people in (Sounds
cool, huh? It is, but we live in a normal, 2,900-square-foot
house not one of the McMansions that are also in the
hood) probably thought we were lesbians, she came here
so much. He would ask her, "You have Dana Duty
today?" Well, Heidi's sister wanted crawfish for Good
Friday, so Jim boiled eight sacks (three hundred pounds),
and we spent the day with their family. It was nice, but I
saw the pain—more of a shock—on her face each time I
looked at her. Still, it was a good day for her, I believe.*

This story has so many layers of meaning. First, there is the
difference Dana's BFF, Heidi, made by being repeatedly present
in the days after Parker's death. Heidi is also a nurse and the
mother of nine children, so she showed up despite her busy life,
as opposed to using her other obligations as an excuse not to be
there.

I have come to believe that people like Heidi were retroac-
tive answers to my own prayers for the Riveras. This sounds illogical, but my heart was so hard-core involved that I found an
appreciation, and thanked God, for the people who had shown
up for Dana before I even resurfaced in her life.

Next, the Riveras' presence for people in a similar situation
made me worry about the effects this would have on Dana's
heart—my main prayer focus much of the time—and made me
realize that these were indeed amazing people I was hooked up
with. I had assumed the Riveras were special—and had told
everyone that—but then the rock-solid examples started flowing

in. The more I got invested, the more I began to see the bigger picture.

Finally, Dana was and is hilarious, even though she's been through hell. Her public aura of positivity and her humor, which have both persisted in an outward-facing way despite her having lost Parker, highlight one of the biggest lessons I've learned from being her pen pal/friend: Grief is not something that goes away or gets better in a certain preestablished unit of time. It is deafeningly silent, lonely, and often goes totally undetected. It never ends. Often, the people with the biggest smiles on their faces are the ones suffering the most.

Letter #217

The recipient of letter #217 was a former Miss Texas pageant winner and the friend of two of my besties, Patty (whom I grew very close to in the fruitful summer of 1991) and Missy—twins from my Olympia days. The twins were also title holders, having won back-to-back Miss Houston pageants in the early 1990s.

Although as friends of the same friends, #217 and I had attended a lot of the same events and therefore interacted, we really got to know each other when we were both bridesmaids in Missy's wedding.

While it was somewhat daunting to literally be photographed standing next to Miss Texas in the bridesmaid lineup—she was number five and I was number six—(who in the hell even thought that was fair?) it also made for some once-in-a-lifetime memories. I remember turning and whispering to her during the ceremony, "I forgot to mention that I was crowned Miss Trinity River Bridge in 1987." She was suitably impressed.

Written in this same vein of awe mixed with humor twenty-five years after we stood together in matching dresses, my words to her may be the single-best paragraph from the entire letter-writing project.

May 16, 2016

The great thing about life is that a fashion-confused girl with a really, really, really bad perm can be friends with a girl who won Miss Texas. They can meet via a pair of dazzling twins and be in the same wedding party, complete with matching belts by Sue Lee, and attend a couple of pageant-watching parties together. Then,

*twenty-five years later, they are still friends via Facebook,
and the one girl (who has now beaten the odds with
superkeratin) loses her mind and writes the other a
meaningful letter.*

Only in America!

Number 217 responded by commenting on a picture I had
posted on Facebook of Will and me at his high school graduation.

May 24, 2016

Hi girl! Got your sweet letter at school today! You made my
day!! Congratulations!

My exchange with #217 was one of the primary reminders
of the best, yet perhaps most underrated, facets of my little social experiment. While, yes, there were lessons to be learned,
feelings to be felt, and concepts to be conquered, the Facebook
project was also thoroughly freaking fun.

Letters #226 & 394

I met the recipient of letter #226 when I was thirteen years old. She was in the cabin next to mine at Olympia—I was in Cabin Athena, and she was in Cabin Venus—for several consecutive summers. Since she was an "older girl" (a connotation that is complimentary only for a limited time) and a popular one, at that, my cabin mates and I were in awe of her.

This sense of admiration continued when she became a counselor before us and then, again, was well liked by everyone. We all, including me, aspired to be her.

I knew that #226 had ultimately gone on to attend law school, practice law, marry a fellow lawyer, and have two children, a boy and a girl who shared her sense of humor. I learned this information not from Facebook but through attending several camp reunions with #226 and her little family.

For her and me, social media kept us apprised of what was happening to friends who not only hadn't seen each other in thirty years but were in touch in a real way, only they didn't see each other regularly.

May 26, 2016

You are one of the few FB friends whom I've known since childhood and whom I've also seen since adulthood and whose kids I've actually met in person.

When I think of you, I think back to being at camp as a camper and how the cabin that you and your people were in was always one ahead of me and my group. You, in our opinion, were the coolest kids at camp, and we all idolized all of you. Then you all moved on and became even cooler counselors, and we continued to follow. It also means we looked up to the same people—our shared counselors. It's an amazing connection.

Fast-forward some thirty-five years (yikes), and it blows me away that we can remain connected through something as abstract as social media—something that wasn't even on our radar in 1982. Sure, it's totally superficial, but without it I wouldn't be able to see how much your kids have grown and achieved since we saw them at the last reunion and I wouldn't be able to see your adventures or read your humorous posts. I enjoy all of your FB biz. So in your case—our case—I am thankful for social media.

More than anything, I want you to know that I still think you are one of the cool kids and that I value your actual friendship. I sincerely care about you and your people and about what's going on in your world. It's all stuff that can never be quantified by "likes" or comments.

Until we meet again (can't wait!), lots of love to you and yours.

Amy W. D.

Your friend in REAL life

Sorry so sloppy.

While I never received a reply to my letter, #226's name did come back up in another way that made her unique among all the other recipients in the history of the project.

When I had initially transferred the names of all of my

Facebook friends onto an Excel spreadsheet and then cut them out individually to place in the box that I'd eventually pull each name back out of, I got sloppy. Because the font I used for the list was small, the slips of paper containing each name were narrow. Number 226, whose married name started with a letter that is found very late in the alphabet, would have been one of the last slips I cut. I assume that by this point, five hundred–plus names in, I was over it and rushing to finish. I know this because the slip of paper containing #226's name was cut in half diagonally, so I could see only part of her name. When I attached the slip, after writing her, to the front of the copy of the letter I sent her, I never stopped to think about where the other half might be.

Well, obviously, it was still in the box. Five months later, in October, I pulled her name back out for a second time. And instead of remembering that I had already penned my real-life friend a heartfelt letter, I wrote her another one.

October 24, 2016

I love how not only are we friends from 1983, but we've seen each other since then and I actually know your kids! Speaking of that, where is your daughter going to school? She must be a couple of years in now. Wow! That's scary. And what about your son—he's an upperclassman in high school? That's the one really great thing about Facebook—staying somewhat updated on real-life friends. I so loved meeting your kids at the reunions, seeing their epic personalities onstage. So, yes, in our case, social media is a good thing!

I can't believe that technology has made it possible for two girls who spent the summer with a tetherball pole separating their cabins to keep in touch. It's a wonderful world!

Until we meet again, I sincerely wish you and yours nothing but joy, love, and peace. That said, I get that these are real lives we're living, so I hope yours is more wonderful than difficult.

Love to you, friend!

Amy W. D.

Your friend in REAL life

Sorry so sloppy.

The only thing that saved me from not officially making the recipient of letter #226 also that of letter #394 was a master spreadsheet I had, which tracked all the letters and replies. I caught the error when I entered #226's name into the spreadsheet and Excel helped me by auto-filling a name I had already used.

It genuinely upset me that I had completely forgotten having written #226. These were supposed to be meaningful letters, which meant they should mean enough to me, the author of them, to at least register somewhere. Even in my subconscious.

I questioned how successful my endeavor to "treat each Facebook friend as an individual" was. One of these valued, cherished humans—one of *my* people—had slipped my mind in a matter of a mere 180 days.

However, given that I wrote another 168 letters between the two, why would I have remembered writing #226 the first time?

Eventually, I came to understand that the letters I was going to remember writing were to 1) people whom I saw regularly in "normal" life, in which case seeing them physically would remind me of my words, 2) people with whom I had some deeper connection or internal conflict that made their letters exceptionally satisfying/difficult to write, or 3) people from whom I had received a response that had thereby turned a one-sided communication into a conversation.

This near miss speaks directly to the inherent impossibility of being friends with more than five hundred people. It just isn't doable. We can love them, we can care about them, we can remember them, but as far as being in an actual relationship with them goes, it's not happening. Not because we don't want to, but because we simply can't.

Letter #266

The recipient of Letter #266 was one of a handful of Facebook friends with whom I couldn't remember how we were connected. I had assumed she was a high school friend or someone I had known growing up. Those relationships were the oldest, and therefore the ones I remembered the least, especially if the person in question and I weren't super close when we did know each other.

The week before I pulled #266's name out of the box to write a letter to her, I had seen something she had posted on Facebook asking for prayers for her family, as her husband was having heart surgery. I didn't comment, but her name kept coming up in my prayers. It was almost like God was "pinging" me to pray for #266. So I did, all the while thinking that I was praying for my old friend from adolescence.

When I did draw her name from the box, I thought, *What great timing—now I can tell her I'm praying for her!*

Even though I was fairly confident that I knew what to say in the letter, I still went and visited #266's profile, because that was what I did before every letter, regardless of how well I thought I knew the recipient. Eight out of ten times, I'd find something that surprised me, which made this review an exercise in understanding that I didn't know people nearly as well as I thought I did. It was one of the most impactful aspects of the project.

In the case of #266, it resulted in my realizing immediately that she and I were *not* friends from school, because we had no mutual friends from that group that connected us. Additionally, she had grown up and spent what looked like all of her adult life in Oklahoma.

The only connection between #266 and me was a mutual close friend, Kristin, with whom I had been a counselor at Olympia in the late 1980s. Kristin was the principal of one of the two elementary schools in the path of the devastating tornadoes that swept through Moore, Oklahoma, in May 2013. I can only surmise that #266 and I became connected in the wake of that tragedy, as we both would have been looped into the same Facebook posts about it as it unfolded. Additionally, I had posted about Kristin during that time, an "I'm so proud to be her friend and am thankful she's safe" status update. It could be that #266 saw that and then friended me.

July 22, 2016

What's interesting about our connection is that we are friends of a friend, in this case of Kristin, whom I worked with at a summer camp in Texas twenty-five years ago and whom you live near now. So you and I get to be connected virtually through Facebook and Kristin, even though we're not connected physically.

The other part that is interesting—and amazing—is that I'm writing you just after I started praying for you after reading your post about your husband's heart surgery.

The way this letter-writing project works is, I draw a name out of a box that holds the names of all my Facebook friends and write that person a letter. You are #266!

What's totally amazing is that even though I didn't comment on your post about the surgery, I started praying for you as soon as I read it. In fact, your name has been stuck in my head. It's like God is screaming, "Pray for HER!" And then—miraculously—I pulled your name out of my box, so now I get to tell you, "Hey! I'm praying here!" ☺

I get that this all sounds a bit ridiculous, but it's true—I'm praying for you, your husband, and your boys. I also hope that you will update us on his condition on Facebook. It's amazing to me how powerful something like Facebook can be, especially since it can also be so wrong sometimes.

I will always think fondly of letter #266 as the Walmart letter. I call it that because I mailed it to the Walmart that #266 worked at, or at least that's what I gleaned from her Facebook profile.

What made our "friendship" and the letter even more extraordinary was that I had been praying for #266 without even accurately cataloging where she fit into my life story. It made her the next in what was becoming a long list of Facebook friends whom I had made erroneous assumptions about.

Though I never received a response, I like to think about where my letter to her went and what it—in the form of God's love—did. Although social media has blurred the concept of what being a "friend" is, it has the power to give us unbelievable opportunities to serve in the capacity of actual friends. To do something—even if it's only once and only for a moment—that has great value.

Letter #300

Letter #300 marked the beginning of my thinking that maybe, just maybe, I really would achieve my goal of writing *all* my Facebook friends a handwritten letter.

While I never stopped and thought, *There is no way I'll actually finish*, I also never told myself, *You're definitely going to write every single person.*

As was the case at the two hundred–letter plateau, I was exhausted and overwhelmed as I reached the three hundred–letter mark, but something was also beginning to turn in me. The letter writing had become a part of me, a part of my everyday life. It had traction. I could feel the momentum building toward a probable—though not definite—scenario in which I gloriously wrote a final-final letter.

The recipient of letter #300 was one of my dearest friends, Dawn Oldham Koenig, one of those life-changing connections I had made at Camp Olympia in the summer of 1991. So not only would I update Dana on the progress of "our" project in that week's letter to her (I can only imagine what I said), I also got super reflective in the three-hundredth freaking letter.

August 16, 2016

So, why am I writing you—or why am I writing every one of my FB people a letter? Well, it all started when I wanted to send my friend Dana—the one who lost her son—a condolence card but realized I didn't have her address—or really any clue where she even lived. It made me wonder what all these online relationships are all about—are they even real? Then, as I continued to write to Dana, I realized that writing her randomly was all about God's love for her—not about me, the great letter writer. The love was so big—and I felt so full and purposeful after writing her, marveling that God was rocking my world via an old FB friend—that I wondered what would happen if I wrote all my FB people. How many addresses would I have? How awkward would it be? Would I even have anything to say? Would it make every one of these individuals seem real to me? And what would my heart look like at the end?

Well, thus far I can tell you I have only about 30 percent of the addresses. Yes, it's totally awkward (sometimes). Yes, I have lots to say. Yes, people are more real after I write them a letter. As for my heart, it's exploding out of my chest.

How many letters have I written? Well, you have the honor of being #300. It's fitting that it's you, and I suppose confetti should pop out of the envelope and you should win a lifetime supply of Rave Ultra Hold hair spray.

In another instance of good timing, I had written #300 just before I knew I would see her at the alumni reunion, which was scheduled for the following weekend at Camp Olympia. While #300 and I were still close, we didn't see each other often, as I was living in Ohio and she remained in Texas. She received the letter as she returned home from camp that Sunday night and replied via text.

August 28, 2016

What a wonderful weekend. I never get enough alone time with you, but look what came in the mail while I was at camp.

You are truly AMAZING. I agree. A gift from GOD. I love you.

I had written three hundred letters in 398 days, for an average of 0.75 letters per day. My journal entry captures what I was feeling: a mixture of awe and excitement and a growing commitment to continue.

We made it to three hundred! HOLY CRAP!

Now, ONWARD!

August 2016

$\mathcal{R}$ight around this time, I received an email from Dana. It came not to me individually but to a group of people who she thought might have an interest in attending the St. Jude Marathon Weekend in Memphis.

Greetings, Team Parker!

If you are receiving this email and were not in Memphis with us last December, I am sending it because I think you may be interested in coming this year. There is a 5k, a 10k, a half, and a full. We also have peeps who come and run nothing—they are just there to cheer us on! If you are not interested, no worries—just trying not to leave anyone out ☺.

Team Parker will once again INVADE M-Town! I have been asked if this will be a yearly thing, and I am just not sure. I do know that everyone in Memphis with us last year felt something ALMOST MAGICAL and said they wanted to do it again this year! So we will go year to year, and WE ARE GOING DECEMBER 2–4. I would also suggest you secure a place to stay NOWWWWW, as rooms sell out!

I also want to give you a heads-up that I and some others will be doing the full and Jim Rivera will do the half. I have not done a full in ten years, and Jim has never done so much as a

5k, but we are facing the challenge like Parker faced all he endured—with COURAGE! So stay tuned! We are honored and humbled at the TOTAL LOVE we feel from so many! Trying to live with FAITH AND ACCEPTANCE, AS OUR PRECIOUS PARKER DID! Hope you can make it to Memphis this winter!

Health, peace, and love,
Dana Rivera

Hard to say no to, right?

Dana had mentioned Memphis in several of her letters, saying that my family and I should consider going. I had replied that if she wanted me to come anywhere, I would be there if I could.

Her email made it real—an invitation to participate in an event that seemed inconceivable on two major counts.

First and foremost were the emotional ramifications. Going to Memphis meant seeing Dana and Jim in the flesh for the first time in thirty years. It also meant meeting their daughters, extended family, and friends for the very first time. This physical reunion, after I had expressed my feelings over and over again in what would have been one hundred letters in as many weeks, would feel like emerging out of the Riveras' mailbox and presenting myself in human form.

As much as I felt an overwhelming rush of adrenaline, I also felt fear—on an emotional level—that was almost unprecedented. The only thing I could compare it to was my emotional state at the end of a meeting my dad had held a couple of years earlier to discuss his will, finances, and final arrangements. It was just he, my sister and brother, and I present. As he wrapped up, he looked at each of us and told us how proud he was of us and how being our father was the best thing that had ever happened to him. I didn't even make it past his third word. I heard him but missed out on his facial expressions as I looked directly at the floor. I was afraid of any external interaction because I had too many deep feelings.

Next were the physical challenges the run itself presented. I had been diagnosed with Lyme disease and Rocky Mountain spotted fever in 2013 and had been undergoing treatment for three years. The Lyme manifested itself in the form of joint issues, numbness, fatigue, and a certain level of mental fogginess. The treatment—a steady flow of strong antibiotics—meant that I also struggled with digestive issues and had periods of time where I could not be in direct sunlight.

When I received Dana's email, my doctor had begun to indicate that I was close to being able to slowly come off the medication, though we had no clear timetable.

I called Willie the same day I received Dana's email, and checked the dates for the race. It was scheduled for the same weekend he was supposed to be in Canada for work, but we decided that I would sign up and that we would work out who went with me, and if I could even run, as it got closer.

I also decided I would attempt the 5k. I could only hope that my rounds of antibiotics would finish in time for me to train. This seemed unbelievable, because not only had I suffered some physical setbacks, I had never been a runner, even when healthy. Cardio had never been one of my spiritual gifts.

I prayed about the entire scenario that evening and then, after sleeping on it, replied to Dana's email the next morning.

I'm IN!
I will sign up for the 5k (definitely the most realistic option). I will likely drive down and will look at hotel options today. I've stayed at the Peabody before but am unsure what else is good in the area.

I can't tell you how honored and humbled I am to be a part of
this. In the meantime, as always, the most important thing is
that YOU are being prayed over each and every day. That
includes TODAY and TOMORROW and all the days that lie
ahead. That's how we do things over here at #CONSTANT.
I'm not going to lie, we're pretty much a legit operation.
Love to you and happy Friday!

Watch out, Memphis—it's about to be ON!

Amy W. D., CPS (certified praying sensation)
#CONSTANT

I hit "send" and freaked out. What if Dana hadn't meant to
include me in the email? How did she even have my email address? What if she was just being nice?

Reaching out to Dana electronically made me nervous on
several different levels. First, an email took our ongoing conversation from the noninstantaneous zone and placed it back in the
modern age. This meant that the sense of freedom I got from
our in-writing link faded as the expectation of an immediate
reply replaced it.

The impact of this shift was compounded by the fact that I
felt—and will always feel—extremely vulnerable with Dana. I
had shared so much with her, and was so deeply connected to
her—beautifully, but not by choice—that I felt exposed. Though
I knew this was all God's business, I was and am still just a regular, messed-up human being.

I went back to work and tried to put it out of my mind. The
good news was, it took her only about an hour to respond.

My family is going to FLIP WHEN I SHARE THIS NEWS!!!
Wowwwwwwwww!

Memphis will never be the same!
Holiday Inn, Sheraton, Crowne Plaza—all downtown, all fine
😊.
CAN'T BELIEVE IT!

Shock and awe descended on me in equal measure. My pulse picked up, and I swallowed hard. But before I could let anything sink in, Dana shot off another email.

Do NOT book a room!
We get two free in downtown Memphis for Friday and
Saturday (for our fundraising efforts😊). One has YOUR
NAME ON IT! You are GOOOOOOOOD for lodging!
WOOHOO!

After thinking, *Holy crap—this is actually going to happen,* my next thought was *Wait! I'm not going to let these people get us a hotel room.*

I mean, somebody else—an actual friend or a Rivera family member—could surely use one of these rooms more than I could. They didn't even know me or my family. Seriously, I was just the ridiculous person writing them letters.

Just a few minutes later, our son Will called. I didn't even ask him what he needed; instead, I immediately vomited out the entire story.

"Mom," he said, "you've got to let them do something for you. You have no idea how the letters have impacted them. They probably want to do something for you, since they feel you've done so much for them."

Though this sounds bizarre to me now, I really hadn't spent a lot of time thinking about what the letters meant to Dana and her family, I think because I understood deeply that I couldn't really do anything for her and her broken heart. While I'm sure the letters were a distraction, as far as any real impact went, it wasn't happening. On top of that, I knew that what I was doing—hunting them down through the US mail and telling them that I (and a team of people whom they didn't even know) was praying for them—was unorthodox. Then there was the total oversharing of my own feelings. None of it was the norm. They had to think I was outrageous—because I certainly thought I was.

And now I was going to meet them. In person. In Memphis, Tennessee.

Letter #316

The recipient of letter #316 was a guy Willie had worked with when he started his career after graduating from college in 1991. Willie and I were just dating at the time. Little did we know, not only would we stay together as a couple, he'd continue working for his first employer for the next thirty years.

Along with #316 and his girlfriend, we were a part of a large group of twentysomethings (and their significant others) who worked together. We did everything from participate in company picnics and softball tournaments to gathering to watch sporting events and cook out. Eventually, we all went to each other's weddings and kept up with a multitude of pregnancies. But as our families grew, our careers took different paths, and relocations separated us physically, we lost touch.

August 26, 2016

Dear #316,

Greetings! I hope this finds you and yours all happy and well. So, first, the obvious question: Why am I writing you a letter? Well, other than clearly losing my mind, recently I've been wondering what it means to be "friends" on Facebook. It all started last year when I wanted to send a FB friend a letter, as her fifteen-year-old son, Parker, had died of cancer. It was a flawless plan —that is, until I realized that not only did I not have her address, I wasn't even sure where she lived. It was a turning point for me. Could I actually be friends with five hundred–plus people without being required to personally invest in most of the relationships? And as much as I loved social media, had it compromised my definitions of words like "friendship"?

That's when I got a truly absurd idea: What if I wrote all of my FB friends a letter? Could it be enough of an investment to redefine "relationship"?

It's amazing to think back on the group of people who worked together at your and Willie's company in the early '90s—young, capable, fun, and just starting out. Now, all these years later, we're all spread out across the country, with spouses and children, well entrenched in lives we could only imagine back in 1992. I feel lucky that I got to be a part of those beginnings, and therefore the relationships, via Willie.

In preparing to write this, I had a good look at your profile—one of my favorite things about the process (digging a little deeper on each person)—and noticed that you've added a degree from Northwestern to those you earned at Michigan and George Mason. I like how that gives you lots of options for sports—rooting for "your" team times THREE. #welldone

It's been a long time, but please know that Willie and I value our long connection with you and your wife and still appreciate your friendship.

As always, I wrote the full letter before worrying about whether I did or didn't have an address. Since we had lost touch with #316 and his family, I had only a vague idea of where he lived. That meant that I started by looking for details on where he worked. Addressing it to someone's known workplace was always the easiest way to send a random letter.

Since there was no such information listed on #316's profile and a Google search was also unsuccessful, I went with the only option remaining and reached out to him via Facebook Messenger.

> Hi #316! Hope you are all well. I was wondering if I could please get a mailing address? I have written you a letter (seriously) and would love to send it to you. I'm not selling you anything, nor do I want you to join my cookie exchange. I'm just writing letters to FB friends in an attempt to make all of these relationships more real. Plus, clearly I've totally lost my mind ☺. Thanks and take care!

Number 316 wrote back, saying:

> Yes, that would be lovely. I really enjoy your FB posts, by the way. Just to confirm this is not a trolling bot suckering me into disclosing my physical address, could you reply with the name of the first supervisor Willie and I had after the operation moved? And then my mailing address is yours for free to spam, exploit via junk mail, or use for drone delivery tests via Amazon Prime—as you see fit!

After I answered #316's question correctly, he immediately gave me his address and I mailed his letter.

Number 316 wasn't the only potential recipient who was hesitant to provide their personal details, nor was he the only one who asked me to prove my identity. That said, it was the exception, rather than the rule, over the course of the entire project.

These instances where individuals questioned my motives was another intriguing facet of Facebook—trusting people's intentions in a forum where "real" relationships are impossible.

All of us, to some degree, use social media—and therefore our online relationships—to "sell" or "advance" something. Whether we're promoting an actual product; an idea; a political stance; an article we agree with; or even a perfect family, marriage, or lifestyle, we have all done it. It's human nature.

The concept of writing a letter for the sake of just writing it —personal, individual contact without an angle, without expecting anything in return—is powerful to the degree that it's almost difficult for us, entrenched in a culture of social media, to get our heads around.

The world would be a completely different place if we assumed that all our friends ever wanted from us was companionship, support, and love.

Letter #324

I can remember vividly where I wrote letter #324: in a hospital waiting room before my yearly mammogram. The letter writing had become such a part of the fabric of my everyday life that if I knew I was going to have a few spare moments anywhere—it didn't really matter where—I brought a couple of letters and my journal with me.

The recipient of #324 was the boys' camp director at Olympia. Not only had he been a friend to me personally since the early 1990s, he had shepherded first Will and then Matthew through the camp program starting when they were young.

September 2, 2016

Most importantly, THANK YOU for investing in my boys since Will started at camp in 2007. Your indelible mark is on both of them, and we owe you personally so much. If you ever wonder what you are doing there, or it gets hard and you wonder if it's worth it, think of all the kids who march into life with camp's influence and protection. You did that; you're doing that; you will continue to do that! #lifechanger

While I never received a response from #324, I did have a series of deep thoughts during the process of writing him. I can only assume that these revelations had to do with my horrible handwriting and my propensity to misspell words. These were deficiencies bound to be overexposed when I penned hundreds of handwritten letters.

I recorded my musings in my journal while I sat on the couch at the Lincoln Park Breast Center.

When you make mistakes in a handwritten letter, people can see them—cross-outs, misspellings, etc.

We live in a world where we can hide our mistakes—edit posts/texts/emails before we send them out.

Letter writing exposes us. It's the "edit-free" zone—that is, unless we want to start over again from the beginning, over and over again, it's the only way to project that we don't make mistakes.

I make mistakes. I guess that isn't only okay—it's okay to let others know.

While presenting clean, error-free copy for whoever might read what we are communicating in writing is a good thing, the ability to filter, edit, and manipulate the rest of our lives can be fraught.

Technology allows us to more easily paint ourselves, and our lives, in shades of perfection. Projecting any mere mortal as flawless, in any way and on any level, is dangerous because human nature demands faults.

Hand-writing a letter, like film photography and live productions, can be made perfect only if the writer continuously starts and then completes the process over and over again until they achieve the desired result, if ever. Not only are we by nature mostly unwilling to do this, it is ultimately unnecessary.

Something that is offered for all to see, even a human life itself, is far more believable, and therefore moving and impactful, if it's authentic. And that includes all the flaws, perceived errors, and beautiful exceptions inherent in real life.

Letter #352

⤧

Letter #352 was to a guy I had grown up with and gone all the way through high school with. We were in band together and had been real-life friends back in the day.

As always, the first thing I did after I drew a name out of the box was sit down to review the recipient's Facebook profile. In the case of #352, the only thing I could remember about what he had done after high school was where he went to college. My lack of concrete memories, combined with the fact that he didn't post much on Facebook, resulted in an eye-opening experience.

Number 352 had landed in California and worked in television. If that weren't enough, he'd just won the second of his now three Emmys for special visual effects for his work on *Game of Thrones*.

I was blown away not only by his achievements but by the fact that I knew nothing about them.

September 22, 2016

First, it seems terribly appropriate to congratulate you on your Emmy award. Wow—I guess I never thought I would say that to you all these years later, but I'm thrilled to do it!

I'm sure you get this a lot, but I'm proud of you. I'm proud that you took all of your awesome talent, intellect, and passion and kicked ass with it. It's an honor to have been part of your past.

Speaking of that, the past, I owe you a thank-you for

*being my friend all those years ago at KOHS. I was
awkward and, like many people at that age, lacking in
self-confidence. You were nice and accepting, and both of
those qualities meant the world to me, especially looking
back now while watching my own kids experience
growing up.*

I never heard back from #352, but the process of writing him was profound in itself, as a part of my continued quest to review all 580 of my friends' profiles.

There were three major takeaways from this necessary task. The term "necessary" is important to understand, because I wasn't scrolling through my friends' details just for fun, or even out of the goodness of my heart. It was a means to an end.

First, I discovered, one friend at a time, that I was connected to an amazing, accomplished, extraordinary group of people. Among my friends list, I uncovered Princeton, Yale, and Harvard graduates; higher-ups in the US Department of State; college professors; A&E executive producers; homeschool teachers; ER doctors; school principals; pilots; foster parents; corporate executives; missionaries; philanthropists; surgical nurses; accomplished musicians, preachers; authors; educators; and even someone who had competed in the quest to be on *American Ninja Warrior.*

Next, I became aware, again, one friend at a time, that I was connected to each of these people for a reason, that we all fit deliberately and beautifully into one another's life stories. It was true whether we'd known each other for thirty days or thirty years. Whether we had spent fifteen years doing life together or fifteen minutes at a mutual friend's daughter's wedding. Whether we shared the same beliefs or lifestyles or political views or not.

Finally, the process of mulling over these extraordinary individuals and their uniquely crafted place in my own life resulted in an overwhelming sense of gratitude. I was, relationally speaking, the richest woman in America.

Being forced to spend several moments earnestly reading each of your friends' Facebook profiles uncovers a gold mine of details and connections that you never knew or have forgotten about. While social media can leave us feeling sad, or pensive, or even downright inadequate when we compare ourselves with others, getting reacquainted with "our people" can also be a life-changing exercise in appreciation that leaves us not only in awe but also happy, nostalgic, proud, and sometimes laughing out loud.

Letter #362

The recipient of letter #362 was Sue Shibley, the across-the-street neighbor at my first house in Ohio. Given that my connection with her had done so much to lay the foundation of how not only to approach Dana and the Riveras in the letters but to engage in the in-writing campaign in the first place, it was an opportunity to merge the seemingly separate narratives into one unbelievable story.

September 29, 2016

I've written 361 of these letters. You are letter #362. It's a big number that adds up to a high level of ridiculousness and absolute heart transformation. I had no idea how many truly amazing people I am connected to and how behind every one of those FB profiles is a beautiful, fascinating, tragic, and wonderful life story. I will never be the same.

Honestly, this is one of the very best letters I get to write, because the truth is, you and your family are the cornerstone of the entire sequence of events that happened prior to this project. And I am confident that God very deliberately connected us.

When we first met, you were suffering—grieving for Lee Sr. I can remember so vividly our many talks—you bravely shared so much. And even though I'm not good at things like comforting, God allowed me to hear your story and be deeply connected to it. One of the many things that so resonated with me was when I watched the video of

Lee and Emma from the grief group. They both said (and later repeated to me in person) that there was a point in time when "the cards and casseroles just stopped coming."

That message changed my heart and path without my even knowing it, because some years later, God gave me a heart for my friend Dana, who lost her son, and when I thought about how to respond to what was an invasion of my heart, your kids' words and yours were loud and clear: Don't let the cards and casseroles stop; don't move on. Since I didn't live close enough for tuna casserole, cards would become my medium. And one hundred–plus cards to Dana and her family later, it's my life that has been transformed. I can't speak for their experience, but, if nothing else, I hope they feel God's presence in my #CONSTANT, unending barrage of words!

Beyond that, those letters (cards) to Dana, or God's love for her and her family, have overflowed into these letters, blowing up people's mailboxes with God's love (whether the recipient believes in it or not).

And it all started when my new neighbor stopped by on a bike ride with her kids—still in elementary and middle school—and was brave enough to share.

Sue, you've changed everything.

My words to Sue in letter #362 might be the best real-time summary of what *Dear Dana* and the Facebook project not only were but still are.

In what back then seemed like unrelated events, the Shibleys' becoming our neighbors in Ohio six years before I reconnected with the Riveras online turned out instead to be a series of delicately intertwined, deliberately engineered occurrences that changed the course of my entire life.

It's concrete evidence that seeds are actively being planted as we go through life. Only living and looking back allow us to connect all the dots. Believing that seemingly insignificant, everyday life moments can—months, years, and even decades into the future—wind up being the most meaningful parts of life is the basis of hope.

October 2016

*I*n the fall of that year, I received two letters, both delivered on the same day, from Dana.

Thank you for praying for our friends as well! I'm not sure if I told you about the Vespers, but I teach with Angela and she taught Parker fourth grade. They have a son at LSU and a daughter who starts with Peyt in August. We have been very tight with them and another couple for years—Friday nights, vacations, weekend trips, LSU games. Well, the Vespers have been at our house once or twice a week since we returned from Memphis in '15. We play cards, watch TV, ride the golf cart, eat, drink, hang with our kids . . . They have been our silent warriors, wanting nothing except to stand in the gap with us. Angela comes or meets me at the health club as well. So thanks for praying for them and the Hamiltons, the other couple who both work full-time yet still check in with us A LOT and invite us over just about every week.

The summer was very sad for Jim and me. Peyton was a counselor at King's Camp after we returned from NYC, and with her gone and Parker's birthday, it was just sad. We had people here almost daily, and Amy and Alli [the Riveras' granddaughter and oldest daughter,

respectively] may well move in! We act like we're okay,
but once everyone's gone, it's just sad. Our hearts hurt
constantly. I know Parker is with Jesus and there's a plan,
but I look at others and think, "Why not them?" NOT
that I want anything bad for others—I just really can't
believe it! It blows my mind. I try to act like he's at camp
or practice . . . but then I have to come out of Fantasy
Land.

The second letter was a card, with a picture of multicolored handprints on the front. Inside was a glossy four-by-six-inch photo of Parker.

Amy:

As I looked for an envelope for your letter, I ran across
these cards and this picture. The cards were made for us
to thank people for the overwhelming outpouring of
donations, plants, food, books, pictures . . . Unfortunately,
I sent out very few. We had good intentions but could
never really do it! The front cover is a painting we did in
the ICU with Parker on January 3. He was unconscious,
and that was good, because he didn't really love art.
When I went to grab an envelope, the picture [of Parker]
was right there. It's one of my favorites because of his
smile and the depth in his eyes. It was taken at our
favorite place, the Peabody, around the 19th or 20th of
December 2014. I hope it's ok that I'm sending it to you.

Love you,

Dana

PS: Hope I'm not depressing you.

Even a couple of years after the fact, Dana's words are still physically painful to read and give me a lump in my throat. Then there's the fact that she managed, again, to be somewhat humorous—"and that was good, because he didn't really love art"—amid the worst circumstances imaginable. On top of all of it, she closed with "Hope I'm not depressing you." All these factors combined say so much about who she is and why people are drawn to her.

I remember holding Parker's picture in my hands and feeling like I was living moments that weren't even real. I showed it to our boys, asking them what they thought I should do with it.

"Mom," they said, "frame it and put it by our pictures on the mantel."

And that is where it still sits, Parker at the Peabody in Memphis, in a purple long-sleeved shirt and LSU pajama pants. Next to his picture are Will and Matthew's school photos.

In less than twenty-four months, I had gone from barely remembering Dana and never knowing Parker to engaging in the deepest personal exchange of my lifetime with her and considering his photo my most valued personal possession.

Stepping on the bus to camp.

Joining Facebook.

Friending Dana.

Not having her address.

Parker's picture on my mantel.

There is a significant plotline running through our lives beyond those things that we can feel, touch, and see. We cannot put our hands on it or even explain it, but it is there—an invisible narrative woven in with the one that seems so obvious and mundane.

Being unsure, and mystified, and confident in things that cannot be proven is a splendid thing. Perhaps it's even worth celebrating—the acceptance of the unreal as real—especially in a culture where we seem to have everything figured out.

Letter #367

I met the recipient of letter #367 in high school. Though the details of our time together were fuzzy, when I wrote her she had just recently shared a photo of her and me. It was Halloween 1985, and we were in costume together. While I'm not sure if I ever commented on the picture, it brought back a flood of memories. We had been in band together, but only for a couple of years; I was two years older than #367, and she moved to another state after her sophomore year. Our in-person friendship was brief.

The photo had prompted me to look at her profile to learn more, an act that would have been a lot rarer prior to the Facebook project. It was then that I found out that she had been in New York City during the attacks on the World Trade Center.

October 3, 2016

I had no idea you were in the towers on 9/11. I saw that on your page last month and seriously freaked out. I had wanted to post/message you but felt a bit silly, as we've been friends thirty-plus years and it's been fifteen years since 9/11, so the opportunity to address it in writing is much appreciated (I draw a name out of a box of my FB friends' names each day and write a letter, so pulling your name now seems like no coincidence). Anyway, I'm sincerely sorry and horrified that you were involved but SO THANKFUL you survived. It makes me mad that I didn't know—that I didn't support you at the time. I guess that's the good thing about FB—at least there is a way to know something. I have NO IDEA how you heal

*from something like that—I'm still emotionally disturbed
by the memory of witnessing it, so for you it must be
beyond difficult. Again, I'm sincerely sorry, filled with
concern, and PROUD TO BE YOUR FRIEND.*

Even though I never received a reply from #367, if not for the Facebook project, it's unlikely that I would ever have reached out to her and told her that I cared about her and was thankful she had survived the terrorist attacks.

While I could contend that I didn't contact her in September 2016, when I saw her post about 9/11, because I knew that eventually I'd pull her name out of the box and write her, that simply isn't the truth.

I didn't reach out to her because, even though, in my own words, I "wanted to post/message" her, human nature prevented me from doing so. I cared, certainly, but the "me" in me either forgot or procrastinated or felt like—as I mentioned in the letter—too much time had passed.

The fact that I drew her name the very next month almost seems like God, or fate, or whatever you want to call it, was pushing my hand. While I wouldn't reach out to her within the confines of "normal" life, I could and would do so via the Facebook project. The force that was driving me to write all the letters was so powerful that human nature didn't have a chance.

I'd like to think that the "me" that exists after experiencing the Facebook project—a totally different person than the one who lived before it—would have acted differently than her predecessor. Namely, that if I had found out about #367's 9/11 experience *after* I wrote the last letter in the project, I would not have hesitated to reach out to her and express the same care and concern.

Because the truth is, it's never, ever too late to say you care.

Letter #379

Letter #379 was to a friend I had met in middle school. We played soccer together and were part of a tight-knit group over the several years we were on the same team. The friendship continued after we stopped playing and remained active through high school, but I hadn't seen her since graduation.

October 11, 2016

What would happen if I tried to write all of my Facebook friends a letter? Could it help me to make a deposit in my relationship accounts?

All of that—complete with horrible handwriting and questionable spelling—is how we arrive here, at your letter ☺.

First up, I'm super excited to be writing you. While yes, we haven't seen one another in thirty-plus years, somehow I don't feel awkward at all penning this. It's not something I can say about all of the letters I've written, and I think it's a testament to the kind of friend you were to me back in the day.

I guess junior high and high school was a tough time for most people. I was no exception, and when you look back on it, it becomes clear that certain people, just by being themselves, made it not only better and easier but something, much later, that I can reflect on with a smile. To me, you were one of those people, and for that I very sincerely say THANK YOU!

Now, all these years later, we have children and cars and bills and jobs and lives that back at Hildebrandt Intermediate School seemed like years into our hazy futures. We have arrived at our hazy futures! I will say that I'm thankful for Facebook in cases like ours, because with it I get the honor of seeing your life now—pictures of your son and daughter and of the fun and positive person you still are to your coworkers, family, and friends. It's a privilege!

And the thing I love the most about being your Facebook friend—and pardon me in advance, because this is going to be super cheesy—is seeing your smile. I swear, it brightens my day each and every time I see it. It's timeless —like all those years never happened and we're still hanging out after soccer practice or at a sleepover.

Until we meet again, know that I value your friendship and care about you and your people. Glad that our paths crossed when they did ☺.

I received a handwritten reply from #379 about six weeks after I wrote her.

November 28, 2016

Thank you so much for "making a deposit in your relationship account" with me. I received your letter weeks ago and was very touched by it and have been marinating over my response. You are absolutely right about this weird connection people now have on FB that allows us to be "friends" but not really. It allows us to rekindle memories from long ago, but they don't develop

any further unless we act on them. I truly appreciate your
personal note and your attempt to "act on it."

I too enjoy FB and the way it lets me see that friends from
long ago and from past lives are doing well, growing,
enjoying life, and experiencing the same struggles I am.
However, I suppose most don't know that I would truly be
there for any of them if they needed me, because FB
creates a wall of disconnect.

Number 379's words about how she "would truly be there for [her] Facebook friends if they needed [her]" stuck in my mind. Not only did I wonder if she would really be there for me if I needed something, I wondered if I would be able to do the same for her or my other friends.

I had learned, from writing almost four hundred letters at that point, that I couldn't be there for all my Facebook people daily as a real-life close friend would. But by doing something beyond the letters, even just small things, could I chip away further at this "wall of disconnect"?

It would take two and a half years, but #379 would answer this question for me in a very direct way. Fast-forward to June 2019, when I had just moved back to Houston and was launching my first book at a Barnes & Noble north of town.

I was a first-time author and new to the area. No one had ever heard of me or my book, and I was worried that people wouldn't show up, so envision my absolute awe when I looked up to see #379 walk through the door with my book in her hand. I hadn't seen her in thirty-three years, but she drove the three hours from Austin to Houston, and then back again, for no other reason but to—as she said—"be there" for me if I needed her.

Imagine that: Something as simple as one deliberate act can have the power to transform a relationship from a superficial state to one that has depth and meaning. If only more people emulated #379's kind gesture, the world would be a much better place.

Letter #398

The recipient of letter #398 is still a close friend. I met him at camp in the mid-1980s, and our paths continued to cross as we lived out the next three decades of our lives. He was also someone whom I genuinely respected. He's one of those natural-born leaders people always seem happy to follow. He's friendly, kind, fun, encouraging, and not at all in your face or pushy.

He's also compassionate and humble. A mutual friend told me a story about how #398 and his family had bought somebody in need a car, even though it was a stretch for them (he and his wife were both educators) at the time. In all the many discussions I had with him, he never mentioned it.

By the time I pulled his name out of the box, he was already aware of what I was doing. First, I had already written his wife, another close friend whom I've stayed in touch with. Additionally, #398 and I had an in-depth conversation about the Facebook project at the biannual Camp Olympia reunion in early September.

Number 398 had seen a Facebook post from another recipient, thanking me for her letter. She was a mutual camp friend to whom I had written in mid-August.

August 23, 2016

Something happened today that literally brought me to tears, and I rarely cry. I received the most loving, kind, sincere, flattering handwritten letter from a friend I have not seen or talked with (outside of FB) in thirty years.

Amy Weinland Daughters, your words moved me, and your action moved me even more.

"Who knows what those letters are doing?" #398 told me as we sat together on the basketball court at camp. "Who knows who you've talked off the edge, who's gotten your letter at precisely the right moment? The truth is"—he paused thoughtfully—"we'll never know. . . . You'll never know."

His clear enthusiasm, and almost awe, regarding my letter-writing campaign had a huge impact on me. First there was the fact that I respected and admired him, I knew that his opinion, especially about something like this, which involved people's hearts, reflected truth. Next, I was all up in the weeds of the Facebook project, and he could see it from overhead.

My conversation with #398 happened less than sixty days before I sat down to write him. This meant I could take his letter in another direction, with freedom provided by not having to explain what I was doing to someone I hadn't spoken to or seen in many years.

October 26, 2016

You already understand why I am writing you: because of my outlandish quest to find something authentic in online relationships, make personal investments in friendships, and share God's fantastic, awesome love— whether the recipients believe in Him or not.

So, rather than explain why I'm doing this, I'll give you a brief update. You are letter #398, so I'm about 70 percent through my list. I write 2 letters every day Monday– Friday and take Saturday and Sunday off. It's a lot of work, but the impact on me is incalculable. When I initially transferred the names of my FB friends onto a spreadsheet in the summer of 2015 so I could cut them out and put them in a box, many of them were strangers.

Even among those I knew, in most cases it had been a while and much of the story was missing. Now, almost four hundred actual letters later, looking through my friends list is like flipping through the scrapbook of my heart—I laugh; I cry; I feel awkward, thankful, and full of joy. And my heart, well, it's exploding. It's become a different level of "relationship"—these are my people, and I'm excited to have them!

So, what to say to you, my friend of yore and today? Honestly, you are one of the people in my life whom I look at and just feel humbled that I get to be friends with you. It's not because you own a Chick-Fil-A or ran a camp and a school, or that you married my friend and produced three new friends. No—it's because of the way you treat other people.

You welcome people, you embrace them, you love all over them and have fun with them, and if that weren't enough, you show love and grace—a consistent example that changes people. Knowing you has changed me— because how can seeing God's love in action not change someone? You've enthusiastically been my friend through the eras of bad perms, questionable fashion choices, early marriage, new parenthood, and now, in the season of watching our people grow up into their own versions of us in the '80s. It's a gift. You are a gift.

Number 398 sent me a handwritten reply within thirty days of receiving my letter.

November 21, 2016

Dearest Amy,

*"I made the LIST!!! Guess who I got a letter from?" is
exactly what I said to my wife as I walked in our door. I
went in and immediately read your letter to ME! It was
awesome and touching. You are one of a kind, missy!
Thank you for writing me. Thank you for going old-school
and making a difference in personal communication.
Thank you for being you! I respect you! I love you! And I
am proud to call you my friend! You bring joy and
laughter into people's lives! God and His love are seen in
you! Keep making a difference in this world to the people
who are around you.*

There is no way ever to gauge how the process of writing the
Facebook letters changed me. My reference to my friends list as
a "scrapbook of my heart" is a testament to how my entire emotional state was upended and then redesigned. It was like seeing
all the same stuff when I looked around me, only it all seemed
brand new. It was like watching football on regular television for
forty years and then suddenly one day watching it on a high-def-
inition, 1080-pixel flat-screen.

The truth is, anyone could have written the Facebook letters. While it's clear that some higher power served me an extra
dose of determination and persistence, everyone has these same
sets, and subsets of relationships, in one form or another. And
even if all the feelings, and their twists and turns, aren't the
same, the results would have been remarkably similar, regardless
of who got to write the letters.

This is everyone's story. Mine and yours.

Letter #400

Letter #400 was the next big milestone in the project, which had dominated the landscape of my life for almost a year and a half at that point. I had written four hundred letters in 470 days, notching my pace up to 0.85 letters per day.

By the time I got to the four hundred–letter plateau, I was completely committed to finishing. I knew it was going to be tough and that I would have to push myself, but I was going to get there eventually.

I remember flipping through my journal or scrolling down my spreadsheet in awe at the volume of communication that I'd achieved. Despite all the goodness that was surging through my emotional canals, I beat myself up for missing writing days, for not responding to replies, and for not wanting to write any more letters.

Then there was the fatigue associated with sharing my feelings and then digesting other people's emotional replies. As much as the process, the exchange, the transaction was so fruitful, it was also wearing me out physically. My hand hurt constantly, and the callus that had been at two hundred and three hundred letters was now huge and stung when I put my pen against it.

All this makes the fact that I was still accepting (though not initiating) friendship requests at this time fascinating—and maybe a bit irrational.

During the fall of 2016, I added twenty-two friends, ostensibly extending my letter writing campaign by that many days.

While, yes, I was feeling "done," I also understood somewhere deep down inside, in a place that wasn't linked to my "doneness," that what I was doing was a once-in-a-lifetime opportunity. I was going to include as many people as I could and press on, because this was, despite how I was feeling, my great destiny.

I was back to that sense of being 100 percent sure of nothing but the letters—these and the ones to Dana.

The recipient of letter #400 was a friend from church whom I saw often. Not only did we attend the same service, she had taught our younger son swimming lessons, our older boys were in student ministry and had played football together, and we all participated in the same Boy Scouts troop.

October 27, 2016

This letter—your letter—is unique because you are an in-person friend whom I actually see regularly in real life. It's not that my other Facebook friends aren't real (especially after I've written all these many letters); it's that I know more about their current situations from posts/pictures than from actual interactions. I wonder what percentage of each person's Facebook friends list is made up of people we see regularly.

The other exciting fact associated with your letter is that it is benchmark #400 on my journey through my friends list. So I suppose confetti should fly out of the envelope, or you should receive a prize—like a dozen Bic pens.

While I didn't receive a written and/or electronic response from #400, we did discuss her letter when I saw her two Sundays later at church.

"I keep checking my mailbox," she told me.

"Hmm . . . for what?" I replied, thinking that surely she wasn't expecting *another* letter.

"For my Bic pens—I'm number four hundred," she replied, laughing.

November 2016

*T*he first week of November, I received two letters from Dana, both postmarked the first day of the month. The first was a response to Will and Matthew—who had thought it would be a good idea if Dana and I each shared five things about ourselves that we hadn't mentioned before. I had sent my five things to her in a card that the two of them had picked out themselves.

She began her letter by saying, "Please tell your boys I loved the card and here they go," and then listed her five things:

1) I have run eight marathons.
2) I am addicted to decorating.
3) I love my job and my school.
4) I am always on a diet.
5) I have met lots of celebrities.

Because my sons instigated the list, I decided I'd share Dana's reply with them. It was the only letter that I read aloud, in its entirety, to my immediate family. I remember vividly all of us sitting in our family room as I read Dana's response. At the beginning, it seemed like a solemn event, reading the words of the person we were all praying for because she had lost her son. Just as I hadn't been revealed in living flesh to the Riveras, we also didn't know Dana in the physical realm yet. This was especially true for Willie and our boys because they hadn't been exchanging letters, and therefore thoughts and feelings, with Dana.

I love my job and my school, I have been at Broadmoor eleven years, and it feels like home. I am the official cheerleader and plan four really big-deal, good-behavior pep rallies each year. The younger kids see me in the hall after the first pep rally and act like I'm a movie star. They're like, "Hey, there SHE is!" I am supposed to be at work at 7:40 a.m., but almost daily I pass my principal at 7:45-ish with coffee in my hand and bid her good morning. She has never said a word and has been nothing short of total support and love through all of this. She also loved Parker ☺.

Dana's ability—in writing and in person—to combine levity, dialogue, vivid descriptions, and thought-provoking material into a single narrative draws people in. I could see the early stages of this impact on Will and Matthew as I read her words to them. On the one hand, they laughed out loud; on the other, they also walked away from the experience having learned something.

It was, in fact, their very first interaction with Dana.

She began her second letter by thanking me for a card I bought in Cleveland, where I had visited with Will after the 2016 Republican National Convention. As was now my practice, I was always looking for cards for Dana, so even a short trip was in part a quest for something new to send her.

She used the unique theme of the card as a starting point for a discussion on her political views, for the most part founded on her experience as a teacher. It's key to remember that, at this point, we still hadn't spoken in thirty years, and since we also weren't doing two-way instantaneous communication, we could both pick whatever topic that came up and then go with it. For the most part, we didn't even have a clue about where the other person stood on any issue.

After twenty-five years, I know this: We are all the same. Children don't see color or religion—they see a playmate at recess. There are those parents who don't care, won't show up, won't pay fees, provide supplies, or even get their kid up for school. For those, the teacher (at least at my school) buys supplies, does the project at recess, gives the kid an alarm clock, uniforms, supplies, whatever is needed.

Dana closed the letter with words that, once again, humbled me to my core.

Amy—you are sharing the light of Christ that could only be ordained by God himself. I don't understand it, nor why we have to walk this path, but I do know Parker knows about this, and I know that one day we will understand. Until then, know that every word you write matters!

Love you,

Dana

Regardless of what Dana and I hoped our words would do for each other, the process of writing about our lives—sharing all the little and big details, the main and supporting characters—had a way of putting things in order.

My letters to Dana didn't only give her a window into my world; they allowed me to view my own life from the outside. Writing it all down, within the safe and freeing confines of non-electronic communication, gave me the opportunity to connect dots that I didn't even know needed connecting. I can only hope that for her, our pen-palling has spawned similar results.

Communicating regularly and honestly in writing with another human being can change your perspective on every single aspect of your life.

Letter #420

⤜⤛

The recipient of letter #420 was a friend from high school. We were in the same class and had sat near each other in band. We had been together all four years and had hundreds of shared memories.

November 5, 2016

You and I both have lots of high school friends on FB, which I believe is a gift. How else in the world could we "keep up" with this number of people? That said, the truth is, I was actual friends at KOHS with a smaller number of people than I'm friends with on FB. I want you to know that you are one of those actual friends and how much that means to me. High school—like real life—was difficult and fun and confusing and amazing. You were such a kind, loving friend to me—it seriously made such a difference. Because of you, KOHS wasn't just bearable, it was enjoyable. I don't know how to thank you for that.

All these years later, I feel honored to have seen your life and your children (beautiful!) via FB. I also LOVE how authentic you are, sharing the good and bad and giving us the opportunity to pray for you—it's inspiring! I also get that these are real lives we are living. So, yes, while we ARE blessed, real life—like high school—can be amazing and messy all at the same time. I sincerely hope your version of life is more joy-filled than difficult.

Number 420 sent me a handwritten note, in the form of a thank-you card, about two weeks after I wrote her.

November 19, 2016

Imagine the surprise of getting a letter from you—at work, no less! That was so nice. I have been thinking of stopping using Facebook, but I am not sure I could keep up with everyone without it now. . . .

Our "little group" of band friends was important to me. It helped me through high school emotionally, as I was pretty much on the shy side. Y'all helped me "come out of my shell" and gave me confidence in myself. So I thank you for being part of that.

I don't have a "best" friend since my cousin passed away almost twenty years ago. Besides my husband, I really don't have a friend to lean on. Facebook friends are the closest I have, and I don't tell them everything, of course, but I know prayer works, so I use FB to ask people to pray for me!

Number 420's revelation that she didn't really "have a friend to lean on" made tears well up in my eyes. It was especially poignant given that she was sharing this intimate detail with a person who had written her a meaningful letter and signed off with "Your friend in REAL life."

Once again, I came face-to-face with the interesting duality of the letter-writing campaign. Though the old-school communication engendered lots of warm feelings and love—to a life-changing degree—on the flip side, I was opening doors that I couldn't keep open.

So many of the responses I received included an old friend

sharing deeply personal specifics about their life. While I accept that this is a compliment to the letters themselves and speaks to the power of the project, on the other hand, it was sometimes devastating.

People shared because they felt special. The letters—not so much my words as the fact that they were an act of treating people like individuals—compelled the recipients to share. They felt as if I truly was their "friend in real life." And though I was, and certainly felt that way, there was no way I could sustain the flame that I'd reignited when there were 580 actual people on the receiving end. It made me wonder how many friends I could really be "in relationship" with.

I came to believe that the answer is a lot like a sleep number bed. Where you might want your side of the mattress to be firm —let's say you're a 65—I want mine to be soft, like a 35. In the same way, you might be able to be in active relationship, and keep up, with twelve friends while I can handle only five.

While there is no "right" number, it's important to know ourselves well enough not to get overextended and spread our friend capabilities too thin. Because while we can't be friends with 580 people, we do have a capacity to solidly show up for, and make a difference to, a select number of friends. And they can do the same for us.

The result is having the capacity to care and therefore be cared for. To support and be supported. To love and be loved.

Not only is that something, it's everything.

Letter #431

Precisely three weeks before Willie, Matthew, and I were scheduled to drive to Memphis, I sat down to write my daily Facebook letters. At this point, fifteen months into the project, I was writing two letters each weekday and then doing any necessary catching up on Saturday. Sunday was my day off and the day that I wrote my weekly treatise to Dana.

The first name I pulled out of the box that Friday morning was that of a camp friend whom I was still in touch with regularly. It was an easy letter to write. When I pulled out the second slip of paper, I read the name and gasped. Dana Dugas Rivera.

November 11, 2016

Dear Dana,

Hi, friend! Well—though I shouldn't have been—I was almost shocked when I pulled your name from the box of options to write a "Facebook letter" to. I guess I thought your name was in there—because why wouldn't it be?— but still, it was a surprise!

I'll start with an update on this project—something I will always consider "our" endeavor. YOU are letter #431— that means I'm approximately 73 percent of the way to my goal of writing everyone. Letters have gone out to thirty-plus states and five different countries besides the US (the UK, Spain, Belize, Guatemala, and Panama). So this thing is literally stretching across the globe.

As much positive feedback as I've gotten, the thing that has changed the most is my own heart. It has altered the way I look at almost everything, and I can see God's hand all up in every part of my life.

But it's key to remember that the series of events of the letters DOESN'T happen without God's love for you and your people. So—again—this isn't a case of me being awesome or amazing (though I'm highly alluring, #clearly); it's about God being awesome and amazing. I won't pretend to be able to explain it all or to know for sure what this all means and how it happened, but my humble take on it remains this: God's love for you and your people got inserted into my heart, big-time. In writing you letters, I started to wonder about social media relationships. I didn't even have your address. I wasn't even sure precisely where you lived. Then this love —which I couldn't be credited with—was so BIG that it oozed out into the idea of writing everyone. What would happen if I did that?

Every one of the letters is the story of you, and me, and God's love literally waking me up in the middle of the night. Whether OUR recipients know it or not—or believe in Him or not—it's God's love that's in the envelope. (Well, at least the good parts—the messed-up stuff is on me.)

It's ridiculous, and it doesn't make any sense. But, in the wise words of my pen pal, "neither does Jesus." #dropthemic

After I drew your name, I thought about how my FB letter to you would look if we didn't have our in-writing relationship (which, in my opinion, is impossible— because without YOUR letters, there would be no FB project). If that were the case, I'd tell you that over the thirty years that separated us after our brief time at camp, I never could get your name out of my mind. Every once in a while, it would pop up: "I wonder what happened to Dana." And that's how I sent you a friend request—during the one moment when "Where's Dana?" coincided with my being on FB.

I would also have told you that although I was fuzzy on the details of 1986, you must have had quite an impact, because you had been tucked away in my head and heart ever since. I would likely have thanked you—sincerely— for befriending a young person with a bad perm and parachute pants. I would have said I was thankful not only that our paths crossed then but that we had FB in 2016, so I could see the life that you and Jim have made together.

I would have said that I understood (through writing more than four hundred letters) that we were both living real lives—which meant that we faced not only the concrete blessings but the inevitable messy, hard stuff. I would have told you that I sincerely hoped that YOUR version of real life was more joy-filled than difficult.

But, as I said, that letter was impossible, because rather than your being just "Letter #431," YOU and YOUR FAMILY are the reason there is a letter #431.

Willie and I sometimes laugh about just how inconceivable the FB letters are. But I'm committed to finishing, sometimes dragging myself (literally) to the next letter. Where it is going, I have no idea. But rest assured and be forewarned that my ten thousand words (misspelled and poorly written) and I will keep you updated.

*In the meantime, WE PRAY—I PRAY—that each of these
letters is yet another avenue to be reminded to
#CONSTANTLY lift you and yours up.*

*I almost want to apologize for all of this—it's ridiculous
—and I get the parts that REALLY make no sense, but
I'll not, and will instead be enamored by our connection,
which, though categorically ridiculous, is BEAUTIFUL
beyond measure.*

I'm praying. And I love you!

#CONSTANT

Amy W. D.

Of the literally hundreds of letters I've written to Dana, this is the only one that I have a physical copy of. I can remember sitting at my desk and sobbing after writing it. It felt like taking a huge gulp of a potent feelings cocktail. Perhaps it was more like scotch than any other liquor. Like physically running into an overtly hot guy in a kilt. The collision is so violent that it knocks you to the ground, resulting in his chivalrously extending an arm to help you back up. It hurt badly and felt amazing all at the same time.

Then there was the "coincidence" that I drew Dana's name a mere twenty-one days before we were due to reunite in Memphis. As surprising as that was, the topic of "great timing" had come up so frequently during the letter writing that I knew it was likely more than just a twist of fate.

Maybe it was a direct answer to prayer. An extra, bonus opportunity to say something to Dana in writing before I had to find words to say to her out loud. This made sense because my prayers had ramped up in the months leading up to the race. I was training to run, and I was using that time, not by design, but out of necessity, to talk to God even more.

Though I had stopped taking some of the medication for my Lyme disease, I wasn't completely out of the woods physically. That, combined with the fact that I had never, ever been a runner, meant that the training was a legitimate struggle. I hadn't planned on turning to prayer when I felt desperate, especially late in my runs, but that's precisely what happened.

Sweating profusely and gasping while other runners passed me again and again—a stiff mental challenge for my competitive nature—I was absolutely sure I couldn't go any farther. Not only did turning my focus to God get me through the next lap, I prayed in a way I never had before. Being depleted physically seemed to augment me spiritually.

It was almost as if God had scripted it, had engineered my signing up for the run—something I would never have done for anyone but Dana—so I would struggle and therefore pray for her and her family even more.

All of it—the timing of Dana's name coming out of the box, my "running," our reconnection, the Facebook letters—pointed to the existence of some kind of higher power. While each of us individually must identify this force in our own very personal way, universally speaking, something out there is bigger than we are.

Letter #441

✳

The recipient of letter #441 was a guy who had very briefly dated my sister. The relationship—theirs, not ours—occurred approximately seven years before I wrote #441 a letter. I know that only because I became friends with him in March 2010. I believe our Facebook connection came to fruition because we were both planning on working at the same golf tournament—he as a caddie and I as a writer. We have never met in person and have never spoken.

November 15, 2016

You are obviously unique among my FB friends because of our connection—you dated my sister, and we became Facebook friends. In my opinion, that's a GREAT opening line for a relationship!

A few things:

1) Thanks for never unfriending me—an option you clearly had, especially after moving on from my MUCH OLDER sister (much older = eighteen months).

2) Honestly, I enjoy following you on Facebook as much as —if not more than—most of my other FB people. I've always felt (via our posts/shares/comments) that we have a similar sense of humor that would be completely revealed only if we went out for drinks with our significant others and perhaps participated in shenanigans and tomfoolery. #yes!

3) Our connection calls into question, again, in my opinion, the very definition of "relationship." Yes, our link is 99 percent electronic, but does that make us less connected than somebody I played soccer with in sixth grade? I'm friends with both of you, but what's real? Perhaps "real" is a shared approach and appreciation for life; perhaps—like a pen pal from back in the day (hopefully with better handwriting), one can be "friends" with someone without sharing the same space.

Therefore, in closing, thanks for being my FB friend. I truly enjoy OUR connection, regardless of its technical definition. See you on the line!

My words to #441 seem to flow easily, as if I were super comfortable writing him despite our weak link. This likely had to do with the fact that I felt like we "got" each other from a humor standpoint and, perhaps even more so, that after writing so many letters, I was on a roll. I could write anyone a letter.

Though I never got a formal reply from #441, we've continued to laugh at, comment on, and like each other's posts on Facebook. In the process, I learned about a year after my letter to him that his brother was in a serious accident that left him fighting for his life.

Although #441 and I are connected via a brief relationship that never went anywhere, it turned out that his brother and I had a more viable connection in the form of mutual high school friends. Our paths most likely crossed, without our even knowing it, in the 1980s.

The intersection of the two relationships meant that when I saw #441's Facebook post about his beloved brother's tragic death in November 2019, I felt compelled to comment on it.

No words good enough—profoundly sorry for you and your family.

Number 441 wrote back:

Well, I was expecting more from a future Pulitzer Prize winner, but I'll take what I can get 😊. Just kidding. I love you.

I'd never even met #441, I didn't know the sound of his voice, and I'd never seen him in human form. We knew we might have a common approach to life, but that was only because of what I had gleaned from social media. He was, after all, "just" a Facebook friend—that is, until I spontaneously wrote him a meaningful letter. And his beloved younger brother died. And I reached out. And he told me he loved me.

For all the concrete limitations of actual human interaction on social media, what if those relationships—the online ones—are or can be as real as or realer than the "real" ones?

Letter #458

Letter #458 was to a girl I had worked with in the adult-beverage industry. We sat right next to each other, with only a cubicle wall separating us, every day for five years. We were, at the beginning, the only two purchasing agents in the Houston branch of the firm we worked for. Together, we were tasked with keeping tens of thousands of products in stock—but not overstocked—in our warehouse. We also handled the logistics of every shipment from all over the world. It was a challenging, stressful, and demanding job.

Number 458 was the perfect person to procure with. She was hilarious, loud, loyal, transparent, intelligent, and hardworking. And, she didn't just have my back when we bought shipping containers full of chardonnay; she was a tremendous friend who saw me through the first part of my marriage, my first pregnancy, and my early years as a mom. We did life together under the nonstop buzz of fluorescent lighting. It was beautiful.

November 26, 2016

So, where to start? I feel like I have lots to say, and I'm super excited to be writing you, for the opportunity to express myself to one of the greatest all-time characters in my life story.

1) I LOVE YOU! Seriously. Yes, lots of time has passed and we've had additional kids, jobs, homes, friends, challenges, and joys since we shared the same space, but really, all that changes nothing about the way I feel about you. Please know that I count our relationship as one of the great gifts of my life. Those years in the sisterhood of the traveling wine container were among the BEST ever.

2) THANK YOU for that time that you and Jennifer drove all the way out to my parents' house for my baby shower. I can still remember looking at you and realizing how significant it was and how much it meant that you were there. AND I still have the robe that y'all gave me. Not to be cheesy (but totally to be cheesy), I TREASURE IT.

3) THANK YOU for bringing me bereavement circus peanuts when I was nine months pregnant and my grandfather died.

4) Here's the thing—no matter how much time and distance may pass between us, I'll always love you, care about you, and be invested in your life. You were/are a gift, and you are one of those rare relationships we get in life that we would go back and live again if we could.

While I didn't receive a written or electronic reply from #458, she did call me not long after I wrote her. That conversation, conducted late at night, lasted several wonderful, amazing hours. It allowed us to catch up in earnest.

I hadn't seen or spoken to #458 in fifteen years when I wrote her, but there was nothing awkward about reaching out to her. Taking the time to consider how beautifully she had fit into my life story and the key role she had played made me realize that despite any deficiencies I saw in my own life, I was a wealthy person beyond measure, relationally speaking. The right people had been there at the right time, again and again. It was a theme that had started early and was still going strong.

It's never too late to say thank you. Doing so has the power to change us as much as, or more than, it does the person on the receiving end.

Memphis

I wrote the last two Facebook letters for the month of November on Wednesday the 30th. Two days later, Willie, Matthew, and I got up early on Friday morning, December 2, and made the eight-hour drive to Memphis for the St. Jude Marathon Weekend.

I didn't write any Facebook letters on Thursday, December 1, assuming that on the morning of Monday the 5th, I would pick back up where I had left off.

I had completed my training the week before the race, finally jogging a complete 5k in about forty-five minutes. It wasn't pretty or even quasi-athletic, but I was fairly confident that I could "run" the entire course.

What I was not even semi-assured of was my impending reunion with Dana and Jim. The fear, because that's what it felt like, manifested itself physically as a tightness in my chest. It was a topic that took over my thoughts and prayers and dominated my conversation with everyone. Anyone I had any level of contact with at the time knew all about it. I even made the unusual move to reach out to the group of people who were praying for the Riveras (Team #CONSTANT, which for the most part consisted of those individuals who had filled out a Praying for You Profile) and asked for prayers for me as I jogged not so boldly into the unknown.

One friend responded by text, *I'll be praying for you! I have your name on my fridge so I won't forget.* She included a photo of the sign on her refrigerator: PRAY FOR AMY! SHE'S A ROCK STAR BUT NOT A GREAT RUNNER.

My BFF in Ohio, Mary Barr, who'd been by my side through the entire Dana story and the Facebook letters and even trained with me for the race, posted on my Facebook page.

> It's too late to text you, so I will write on your wall. Forty-three minutes of absolute awesome. I love you and I know you will be forty-three minutes of strength and grace and love. And constant-ness. Praying from here.

After nine weeks of hard-core "couch to 5k" training while still on medication, my body was in shock. Who did I even think I was? The first time I'd run all five of the k's, I'd legitimately felt —in my own head—like an Olympic athlete. I hadn't just heard the *Rocky* theme in my ears; I had it on my playlist. But my body must have been thinking, *C'mon, girl, get back on the couch. Where are the freaking Cheez-Its?*

Next, my mind was in shock. I felt like I was going to have to "answer" for my emotional escapades. As if it were "judgment" time and the Riveras were somehow going to call me out for all my sharing. For all the commentary I had no business commenting on.

I had even written about Parker. At the beginning, I hesitated to mention him at all, knowing full well that I had zero business discussing Dana's precious child. As I talked further with God and got more entrenched with the Riveras, I began to realize how much Parker's relationship with Jesus had to do with my connection with Dana. Even as I got that, sharing it with her in the letters was perilous for me personally. I would ask Mary Barr what she thought before I said things I felt nervous about. Even after her resounding support, many times I put a letter in the mailbox at the post office and thought, *Oh, dear God, what have I just done?*

I can distinctly remember not knowing what I was doing but not being able to stop doing it. That's the only way I can explain it.

On top of all that, I wondered how Willie and Matthew—much less I—would fit into the Riveras' situation. How was that even going to work? While they were committed to going and seemed excited about the trip and the reunion, they hadn't yet made the deep spiritual and emotional connection with the Riveras that I had.

I can remember telling Willie, "This is one of the biggest things that has ever happened to me in my life."

"Really?" he responded. "I mean, I get that it's huge, but you'd rank it at the top?"

I remember being somewhat flabbergasted by his response. But, that said, and though he'd certainly prayed for and discussed the Riveras, he wasn't a part of our pen-palling and hadn't been gripped by Dana's words. Though we were doing life together, he wasn't having the same profound experience that I was. He really *didn't* know the Riveras. Yet.

I didn't sleep well the night before we went to Memphis, and I was agitated the entire way there. Mary Barr was primed to pray at the exact moment she thought I would prance back into the Riveras' world. One part of me knew that God had it completely, because how in the world had I even gotten involved in this entire scenario in the first place? Coming into reconnecting with Dana, I wasn't even praying on a regular basis and then—boom!—I was suddenly writing virtual strangers about how I, along with a group of individuals whom they knew even less, was praying for them constantly. And about how they should believe that God loved them, despite the fact that they had experienced a depth of loss that I didn't even want to imagine.

The other part of me—the middle-aged, human female and mother of two—was freaking out.

We stopped for lunch at the Cracker Barrel in Jackson, Tennessee. I didn't even think I could eat. That's when I got a text from Dana asking for our ETA. That calmed my nerves because at least she was expecting us; at least it was on her radar. At least we weren't maybe being total freaks.

The Riveras were staying at the Peabody Hotel in Memphis, their home away from home, on the south side of downtown, nearer to Beale Street. We were staying in the hotel room they had generously provided us to the north, toward the convention center and St. Jude.

In her text, Dana said she had checked us into our room and that all we needed to do to get our keys was show our IDs at the reception area.

When we finally arrived, we approached the reception desk and I gave the woman working there my name and ID.

"I know who you are!" she exclaimed almost emotionally. "And I know what you've done. I know about the letters!"

If that weren't enough, rather than just passing the room keys over the desk, she came around the counter and hugged me tightly.

"Thanks for everything you've done," she said.

I felt like I might literally pass out right there.

Dana had obviously shared our story when she had checked us in. Though I got that, this was a giant hotel on the busiest weekend in Memphis—so how in the world had I waltzed up to a check-in counter where four employees were working and magically picked the same person Dana had spoken to?

Next, this was the first time I had heard directly from a third party that the letters and pen-palling were such a big deal in Dana's world. I supposed I could have assumed that, but I didn't. Inside my own head (where assumptions, emotional obliviousness, and low self-confidence ruled the day), I had, from the very beginning and perhaps even now, seen the letters as somewhat bizarre, totally unnecessary, and perhaps even a pesky nuisance. Plus, seriously, what could they really do, given that Dana had lost her precious Parker? It made the fact that she would have told a hotel clerk the entire story almost surreal.

The other thing I didn't get yet, which also partially explains the clerk's enthusiasm, is that the people of Memphis are all in for St. Jude. We would visit Memphis for several more marathon weekends, and each time we were made more aware of the special relationship between the city and its famous hospital. The lady at the front desk of the hotel on this Friday, December 3, was the first of many people—from nurses to bathroom attendants to Uber drivers to bartenders—who displayed a family-like passion for St. Jude.

Putting myself out there for the Riveras on an unprecedented level left me in a position of fear. What I learned that day, and weekend, and afterward, is that it's okay to give even when it's scary.

There are moments in our lives when everything inside us tells us to do something that defies logic, that derails our own plans, and that we know will seem ridiculous to others. When we opt to push logic aside, ignoring everything but that one voice, and follow through on that special something, suddenly everything can change in a way that we never even thought possible.

The next surprise was waiting in the room itself: a huge basket filled with Louisiana, St. Jude, and Team Parker treats sitting on the counter. There were Louisiana potato chips, beer, Mardi Gras beads, St. Jude cowbells, Team Parker stickers, etc.

There was also an envelope containing several items, including a note from Dana.

#ConstantFamily!

Welcome to M-Town, aka Memphis! We had only been to Memphis once before diagnosis, but it soon became our favorite place to be. You guys have NO IDEA how very humbled we are you are here. THANK YOU!

I've put a lil' "sussie" together for ya! The food products and beer are all LA made! The Christian Youth Theater shirt and mug are there because Parker LOVED CYT. They have a scholarship in his honor. The other things are just lagniappe (LA talk for "extra"). I hope the obituary and funeral cards don't freak y'all out—it just seemed right to include them. The Christmas card was the one we were sending out in '14 before we found out the cancer was back. They never got mailed. I hope you have an AMAZING weekend. ☺

Love you ALL BIG!

Jim and Dana

The plan was that we would meet up with the Riveras at the Peabody after I had checked in for the marathon at the convention center. Dana had told me to call her once I had completed that task. That phone call, which I made from the hotel room after we had changed into our Team Parker T-shirts, marked the very first time we had actually spoken since the summer of 1986.

Hearing her voice for the first time in thirty years—especially given the thousands of words we had shared in writing—made me want to cry, laugh, and perhaps drink heavily, all at the same time.

"This is weird—we've never ever talked on the phone, not even when we first met," I told her.

"I know," she replied, her voice maybe how I remembered. "This is the first time you've ever called me."

Crap, I thought. *Was I supposed to have called her?* But even I, the perpetual worrier, knew that I had not called her or communicated with her regularly via instantaneous communication for the same reason I, an almost complete stranger, had written her more than one hundred letters: gut instinct.

As we set off for the twenty-minute walk to the Peabody, my nerves went wild. I literally prayed and freaked out every step along the way. The entire unprecedented sequence of events had led to this moment. But, of course, I wasn't talking about it.

That didn't mean that the people I had dragged into the situation weren't aware—a fact evidenced by Matthew's comment as we were about to walk into the Peabody.

"Mom," he said, as he looked up into what I'm sure were my wild eyes, "how does it feel to know your whole life is about to change?"

Wow.

Willie, as always, and fortuitously, took a more logical approach: "It's fine, Amy. . . . They know we're coming, and it will be just fine."

I probably needed someone to scream that in my face. And hug me very tightly.

The grand lobby at the Peabody is as good as it gets. Living up to the word "grandiose" from top to bottom, it shone even more brightly because it was decorated for Christmas. Embellished with mahogany, marble, and decorative iron, the main room stretched up two stories, with a balcony on the second floor that lined the perimeter of the entire space. At the center was an ornate fountain topped by the largest fresh floral display I'd ever seen. At one far end of the rectangular space, dotted with cozy couches, chairs, and tables, was a perfectly decorated Christmas tree that stood a full thirty feet high. At the other was a stately bar surrounded by happy patrons.

We entered the lobby from the end where the tree dominated the room, giving us cover and allowing us to see the Riveras before they saw us. They were easy to spot because we were wearing the same T-shirts and their group was huge, consisting of several dozen people.

They were gathered around a group of couches located on the left-hand side of the room, which meant we could take the marble pathway to the fountain and then turn to greet them.

I didn't hesitate to get directly to Jim and Dana. I zeroed in on them and was pulled in as if by magnetic force. It was all adrenaline. I assume, because I didn't even look back, that Willie and Matthew followed me in, past the rest of the group.

Jim turned to us first. While I could see glimpses of the young man I had met at camp all those years before, his countenance reflected the three decades that separated that time from the present. He hugged me warmly, saying, "Hey, Amy. We're so blessed that you're here."

Dana was next. She looked like her Facebook pictures, but seeing her in person, in live action, took me back to the big personality I had gotten to know and love in 1986. I couldn't get that sense of who she was online.

"Welcome to Memphis," she exclaimed, hugging me tight.

"Thank you, Dana. My heart's about to explode out of my chest," I replied.

"I know," she said, chuckling.

I'm not sure what I pictured. I had certainly envisioned our reunion in the months, weeks, and days leading up to it, but it played out differently than I had thought it would. I suppose I had assumed a bunch of meaningful words would gush out, both of us interrupting each other in a lame attempt to describe what it felt like with adjectives. We would likely cry. Right?

Instead, we didn't say much at all directly to each other. And there were no tears. Because we had already exchanged so many words and even more feelings, more than I think we could even get our own heads around, we didn't need to talk. We didn't need to sob. We'd done that. And so we simply, almost as if by instinct alone, fell into a rhythm together. It was almost like we belonged together, like it wasn't foreign, like we had always had this place beside us where the other one fit.

As incredible, on a supernatural level, as our reunion was, it felt equally normal.

Dana immediately began to introduce me to the crowd. I followed her from person to person as Willie and Matthew went to get us drinks.

One by one, the people she had introduced to me with words took human form. What struck me first was that everyone was referring to me as Constant. I was being presented not as "Amy," or "my pen pal," or "my old camp friend," but instead as Constant. I don't think they even knew that I had a regular name. Additionally, every single person knew exactly who Constant was. There was no need for an explanation.

I mentioned this to Dana, and she showed me her phone, where I was listed in her contacts as Constant.

I didn't even know that was a thing.

Next, I watched as Dana interacted with her people. First, she was large and in charge, almost holding court but in such a way that everyone was on board and seemed genuinely happy to be there. She was loud, hilarious, and engaging. Her big personality, though not a mirror image, reminded me of my own. But then I was reminded of the biggest difference between Dana and me when one of her friends asked her, "What are your plans for Christmas?"

"To just survive it," she replied. "Of course we'll do it all for our girls, but we'll just want it to be over. And when they've all left, we'll just be sad. It will suck." She teared up as she spoke, visibly upset in a way I hadn't anticipated. But then why would I have thought I could gauge how she would react to anything, except for maybe a letter?

"I just freaking hope no one says 'merry' Christmas to us, or 'happy' holidays, or 'happy' New Year," she continued, with more of an edge, but still clearly sad, "because there ain't nothing merry or happy about it. But"—she stopped, softening her tone— "people don't mean anything by saying that; they just don't know, because they can't."

She was so honest. Her voice, her sharing out loud while I was standing right next to her, almost physically incapacitated me. Hearing her talk about how she felt, after not only reading her words about it but praying and imagining what life must look like for her, was almost too much.

We moved to a table near the fountain so we could watch the famous Peabody ducks march from the elevator to the center of the lobby for a quick swim and then back again to their high-rise pond on the roof.

I was given a prime spot in a room that was jam-packed with onlookers. Sitting next to me was Angela Vesper, Dana's teaching BFF, whom she had referred to in her letters—along with Angela's husband, Jason—as the people who stood "in the gap" with them between their old and new lives.

While Angela and I exchanged small talk, I felt the need to tell her how Dana's words about grief had affected me.

"The stuff Dana said," I muttered, "about getting through Christmas . . . That was hard to hear. It floored me."

Angela Vesper is genuinely one of the most compassionate people you'll ever meet. She's also a legitimate straight shooter.

"Yes, that's how it is," she replied, with just a few simple head nods.

Then it hit me: While I'd been dispatching all my letters, Angela and other close friends of Dana and Jim had been on the front lines, dealing with the real grief.

Suddenly, I felt physically ill. This "aha" moment, delivered with a thunderous clap, confirmed some of my initial fears. It came from insight that I couldn't have had from my position at the other end of a letter or a prayer. It was as if everything I thought I knew, including my own place in the story, suddenly spun around—and the truth was, I didn't know anything.

While I'd certainly been praying nonstop, and caring and worrying about the Riveras, I was doing it from the outside looking in. My perspective was all jacked up, not because I wanted it to be but because I was living in my own reality, not Dana's.

It made me begin to understand the absolute inadequacy of my words to Dana. It wasn't that the letters weren't well intended or meaningless; it was that there was no way they could help. And, really, what the hell was I doing, for Dana or anyone else, while people like Angela were really being there?

My confidence plummeting, I got up from the table and

walked over to a chair on the periphery of the group. Sitting down heavily, I replayed the entire sequence of events in my head. *I friended her. I found out about Parker. I went to church. I started writing letters. I kept writing letters. She wrote me back. She kept writing me back. We met in Memphis.* As much as I knew the whole situation was inspired and profound, in that moment in the Peabody lobby, I felt as out of place as I ever had.

It didn't make any sense, and, as a regular, flawed human being I grappled with understanding how I had gotten myself in this deep. Yes, I knew it was God's work, but all I could see, in the foreign landscape I found myself physically alone in, was my own inadequacy.

Just then, as if out of nowhere, Dana approached me. "Let's go, Constant," she demanded, waving her arm. "It's time to move on to the next stop. We're out of here."

I watched as she collected a few more people to make the trek to be the first ones at the Flying Saucer, a nearby restaurant/bar where the full version of Team Parker would meet. I realized she was gathering her closest friends to go with her. She was including me in this group.

Looking back at me still sitting in the chair, she repeated with a smile, "Come on, Constant, get your people—we're going!"

It was as if she sensed that she needed to, or perhaps had been compelled to, reassure me at the precise moment I so needed reassurance. I didn't fit into this group in any way that made any sense, but somehow, I really did.

And so I did what I'd always do: I followed her to the next adventure.

$\backsim$

Jim and Dana had reserved a big room at the Flying Saucer and then filled it with what had to have been one hundred guests clad in gold T-shirts with "Team Parker" spelled out in purple. We took a group photo, were introduced to more of the Riveras' people, drank beer, ate, and watched as Matthew played giant Jenga with one of Parker's nurses from St. Jude. There were so many people there that we never really felt like outsiders. Plus, generally, I don't think anyone feels left out when they're hanging out with people from southern Louisiana. It may even be impossible.

As the crowd began to die down, Dana's four girls were all sitting at one of the long tables. Though I now felt less freakish about Dana and Jim individually, I was hesitant about getting all up in their daughters' business.

But I was compelled to do just that. So I went and sat down with them, four strangers who must have thought I was ridiculous. To their credit, they included me in the conversation, and luckily I quickly realized that we had a similar sense of humor. In discussing the race the next morning, we came up with a new app, called Uber Race, that would allow us to be picked up at mile two and delivered to the finish line. The car would go the same pace we could run, so mine would be like a Ford Pinto being pushed by two drunk people. But of course I couldn't leave it at that.

I felt an overwhelming urge, as if it were my one and only destiny, to tell them, awkwardly, I'm sure, "Hey, listen—I just need you all to know that I really am praying for y'all every single day." They each smiled and thanked me, but other than that, we didn't discuss it. Their response was warm and sincere, but I could tell that they weren't quite sure what to think any more than I was. Like my people, they hadn't been privy to the words Dana and I had exchanged. And they hadn't even known me thirty years ago. I was just somebody who had inserted myself in their mother's life at the worst moment in their collective experience.

This hunch was confirmed in a side conversation with Daughter #2, Lauren, who briefly discussed the letter writing with me after we got up from the table.

"Look," I told her, "I know this is all illogical: the letters, the prayers, the fact that nobody asked me to be involved . . . I get that. But I just can't stop."

"It *is* ridiculous," she agreed, "but I know Mom has said stuff to you in the letters that she hasn't said to anyone else. All I know is, the letters are a good thing."

The next morning, because of the long walk to the starting point and the early start time for the 5k, I woke up at around five o'clock. I remember rolling over in bed to turn off my alarm and immediately thinking, *Oh, crap—now I've got to try to run 3.1 miles on top of everything else.*

The emotional roller coaster I had ridden on Friday had muted my concern about the physical realities of running my first-ever 5k. While I felt a sense of pride wash over me as Willie pinned on my race number, a scene I never could have imagined, it also made me doubt my training and the rationality of my goal to run every step of the race. In addition to my regular state of physical numbness and joint pain, I had a queasiness that I assumed was nerves mixed with a short night of sleep after a long evening of lager.

It was still dark outside when we made our way across town to the starting point. Willie and Matthew, after wishing me good luck, left me in the growing crowd and told me we'd meet at the finish line.

"You got this, Mom!" Matthew called out, before walking away.

The street was jam-packed with participants as far as the eye could see, both in front of and behind me, to the point that, as alone as I felt, the spectacle distracted me in a good way. Eventually, the music cranked up and an early-morning party scene ensued.

As the start time drew near, three of Dana's girls—Mady, Alli, and Peyton—found me, somehow, some way, among the thousands of runners. As if on cue, fueled by the same power that had connected us without our even knowing it, they had entered the throng of participants at the exact point I had. In the same way Dana had been the night before in the Peabody lobby, they were seemingly on call to reassure me.

Mady suggested that the four of us take a picture, which we did. It still overwhelms me every single time I look at it—me and Dana's girls, with our arms around each other, about to run a race that I had absolutely no business running. In Memphis. At St. Jude. After one hundred truly random letters about God's love.

Even as a lover of words, I'll never, ever be able to adequately express what that means.

I didn't try to keep up with Dana's girls, though we crossed the starting line together. This was a decision born of self-preservation. If I was going to finish and run every step, I was going to have to jog. That meant I would have to try to switch off my competitive nature and stick to the plan.

That said, the rush of starting a race with thousands of other people meant that I got off to a faster pace than I intended to. Though I managed to slow down, I worried, as I knew finishing was going to take everything I had.

The first mile seemed to last forever. I could feel on my thighs every taco I had ever eaten, a jiggling enhanced by the uneven roads in downtown Memphis.

Mile two seemed much shorter because it wove through the campus of St. Jude. I'd driven past the hospital numerous times but had never been on the actual site. Patients, their families, and medical staff lined the sidewalks along the course, ringing bells and cheering us on.

They also held up handmade signs:

YOU ARE OUR HERO!

KEEP GOING!

IF YOUR LEGS GET TIRED, RUN WITH YOUR HEART!

RUN, FORREST, RUN!

THANK YOU, HEROES!

One patient, who looked to be about ten, was in a wheel-chair, holding a sign that read IF I CAN DO IT, YOU CAN TOO.

As compromised as my body felt, my spirit was flying. Humbled and crying, I could think about nothing besides Dana, Jim, Parker, and the rest of the Riveras. This was where they had been, down these paths and in these buildings. And I was running through it all while people applauded for me. I don't know that I've ever believed in God as much as I did at that moment.

Mile three felt twice as long as mile one had. It began on one side of what looked like the Golden Gate Bridge only in reality was a two-lane overpass that barely went over Interstate 40. I could have crossed it in ten seconds in my car. On foot, not so much. This was where the beer, my lack of sleep, and my questionable cardio gifts caught up with me. But I trudged on, gasping and hurting but refusing to walk. I was a total badass. Or not.

When I finally turned the corner to the finish line, my old friend adrenaline returned. I was going to freaking do it. I saw

Willie and Matthew out of the corner of my eye, both yelling out words of encouragement, and I lifted my hands over my head.

It had taken me twice as long to finish as the winner in my age group, and I could barely walk, but I had done it. I had "run" every step of a 5k.

Afterward, I hung out with other Team Parker members and then reunited with Willie and Matthew. We ate a late lunch and returned to our hotel room.

Dana texted and said we were going to meet for dinner. Because every other restaurant in downtown Memphis was packed, we ended up at Hooters. The service was slow and inaccurate, but being there, basking in the glow of the orange neon together, felt special. It was also perhaps the only place where someone who had worked hard over several long months to achieve athletic excellence could feel bad about her body by simply comparing herself with the waitstaff.

The Team Parker crowd was down to just family and close friends. I still wondered if we belonged in this exclusive group, but we laughed the entire time. I was beginning to see how, when combined, Dana's and my personalities were like a perfect storm. We fed off each other's energy.

"That reminds me of my first marriage," I told the group, as they discussed something about a couple I didn't know. It was one of my running lines—that and then referring to Willie as either my first or my current husband (even though he was both) was my bread and butter. It confused people, especially people who didn't know me well.

While my remark seemed to have the desired effect on the rest of the crowd, Dana immediately "got it" and launched in.

"Your *first* marriage?" she questioned. "To me, it was *way* more like your third. But"—she paused for effect—"that was an absolute shit show, so we won't even discuss it."

I also shared a couple of hilarious moments with Mady. Those, too, began with our shared sense of humor. Like, who drinks beer at Hooters and fabricates a rapper sighting in the bathroom and calls it sharing God's love for people who are grieving?

We do.

God does.

Sometimes, the fewer rules, the better.

The group began discussing plans to move on to a blues club on Beale Street. I assumed we wouldn't make that part of our evening because we had Matthew with us. But Dana offered up her youngest daughter, Peyton, to watch Matthew because she would also be watching Little Amy—Alli and Jacque's little girl.

I accepted. Willie was shocked because I'd never, ever let somebody I didn't know well watch one of our kids. But this was Dana—she was and is an exception to all the preset rules in our lives. Plus, even though we hadn't had any physical contact, our in-writing sharing meant that I trusted her.

When we first arrived at B.B. King's Blues Club, we grabbed beers and sat on the side of the dance floor. The guys hung back by the bar. I eventually headed out to dance with some of the others while Dana sat and talked to her people.

This produced one of my favorite moments of the weekend, a moment as nonsensical as this entire story itself. As I continued to consume the beers, I lost the few inhibitions I still possessed and began dancing like no one was watching. I'm sure I scared the crap out of my fellow dancers. Eventually I began to slap my own butt and sashay up and down the dance floor. When I noticed that Dana and her friends were watching me and laughing, I amped up my performance accordingly.

This is the moment I like to think of as *Hey, watch me slap my butt, and oh yeah, I really am praying for you and your family.*

In time, we wound up in an upstairs room overlooking the dance floor. We drank more and talked some, but more than anything watched the house band—complete with a full brass section—play.

I was sitting across from Dana, right on the balcony. I thought about how quickly the weekend was slipping away. I had no idea how I had even ended up there or what would happen next, but I sincerely didn't want it to end.

Willie made the call that we needed to go and get Matthew, which made sense, as we had left him with someone we barely knew in a hotel room in downtown Memphis.

Luckily, I had written Dana a very small card, which I had shoved into my back pocket after the race, thanking her for including us in the weekend, for the hotel room, and so on.

We both cried as we hugged goodbye. We were leaving to drive back to Ohio the next morning, so this was it. I put the card in her hand and told her I'd "be in touch." She laughed.

Despite the lack of my clearly defined place in it, the scene was difficult to walk away from. I felt like I was leaving a part of myself behind. It was my heart. It was God's love. It was 11:30 p.m.

Goodbye is just something we say to tide ourselves over. The depth of this specific relationship and others like it means that we're never truly apart from the ones we love.

Lafayette

*B*ack in Ohio, I worked hard to come down from the trip. I got ready for our trek south for Christmas. I wrote football articles. I wrote to Dana. I prayed even more fervently than I had before Memphis. But I didn't write a single Facebook letter. I just couldn't do it. Even though we had been gone for only one weekend, I had fallen out of the rhythm I had been in for months. The combination of the reunion and the run left me emotionally and physically depleted. I needed time to recharge before pressing on.

Mary Barr and I met at Panera the Tuesday after the run to recap the weekend. As much as it had been a success in a bunch of different ways, I told her that I felt like I had more to do beyond continuing to write letters. While my connection with the Riveras was completely unscripted and I had no clue what might happen next, I had never envisioned that Dana and I would see each other in person regularly. That was true even once I knew we were going to reunite in Memphis. I had no expectations.

But now, after seeing Dana, I knew, in almost the same way I was committed to writing the letters in the first place, that there was something beyond our postal relationship. I suppose it had something to do with the epiphany I had after talking to Angela. I was connected to the Riveras for a reason, so why wouldn't I make myself physically available in the real world if I could? It would just require a little more effort because of the great distance that separated us.

As Mary once again played the role of designated driver of my emotional state, I decided to email Dana and, just as I did with my Houston friends each time I went home, ask her if she wanted to get together while we were in Texas for Christmas.

Dana replied quickly and said she was available on Friday, December 23. This was just after she got off work for the holidays but before they packed up directly after Christmas and went to the beach for New Year's. It was one of the most difficult stretches of their emotional calendar, as Parker had relapsed on December 11 and passed away on January 4.

She said she could meet me halfway for lunch but mentioned that since she had returned home after Parker died, she wasn't good with driving long distances, especially on her own. I replied that I loved driving and was happy to come all the way to Lafayette, which is approximately four hours from our place in East Texas.

She invited me to her house so I could see some of the renovations she had detailed in her letters. We would go and eat from there.

We left it at that. I had again ticked a box on my invisible, subconscious "to-do" list. While I was personally oblivious to its existence, completing each task as it appeared was critical to my moving forward.

We had been back in Texas for only a few days when I drove to Lafayette early that Friday morning. I had told Dana I would try to arrive at her house by eleven, which meant I had to leave by no later than six thirty. I spent most of the drive trying to get my head around how I had gone from barely remembering Dana and Jim just three years earlier to ecstatically reserving an entire day of our brief stay in Texas to drive eight hours round-trip for the opportunity to see them.

The other thing that kept popping up was the timing of our reconnection. How was it that I had gotten the big idea to write Dana letters just weeks before Parker passed?

The hours and miles passed quickly, and before I knew it, I was pulling up to the address that I had written on an envelope well over one hundred times. As with Memphis, it was like watching Dana's words magically transform into a physical landscape that I could see and touch.

The first thing I noticed was the Riveras' mailbox, which sat at the end of the sidewalk that went directly from the front door to the street. Almost as if on cue, the postal carrier was delivering the mail precisely as I arrived. Prior to this moment, I'd had no idea that Dana received her mail in the morning. It was like watching a sacred ritual that mattered to me deeply but that I had never witnessed before, or even imagined.

I contemplated stopping the mail carrier and thanking him for his part in our pen-palling. Before this, I hadn't thought to consider that the same person might be delivering my letter to Dana every week. That would make him the conduit, whether he knew it or not.

It made me wonder: What if we're all doing something that seems ordinary and mundane, but in fact we're playing a silent yet essential part in changing the world?

After a long chat with God, I disembarked from my car and walked up to the house just like it was the normal crap that I did.

"Welcome to Laffy!" Dana exclaimed as she opened the door.

The scene inside was impeccable: candles lit, lighting on point, music playing in the background, holiday decorations up and gorgeous—everything in its place. A bottle of champagne was open in a bucket; custom-crafted petits fours were displayed perfectly.

It was obvious that Dana had cleaned her house from top to bottom. I wasn't sure how she had pulled that off after working a full day the day before, after getting prepped for the holidays, after reliving some of her toughest memories.

Though I probably should have acknowledged all the hard work that she must have put into my visit, I didn't. Just as we didn't exchange a flood of words when we first met in Memphis, we didn't dive into deep conversation here, either. It was all about the volume of words we exchanged in the "other" layer of our relationship—the in-writing one.

Dana showed me around the house, the proverbial "tour" that you give to guests, sometimes awkwardly, who have never previously invaded your space. What was different was that she had already described, with words and no pictures, each of the rooms I was now seeing. It was like being inside a book I had previously read.

The last stop was Parker's room. Jim and Dana were in the process of renovating it for their grandchildren to use when they visited. Taking me to the far-right corner, she showed me the part of the room they didn't ever plan on changing, a tall bookshelf that Parker had filled with the things that he held most dear.

My head began to spin, and I felt a huge lump in my throat, not because I knew Parker but because I had two boys of my own, and they, too, had collected a wide array of "specials" and displayed them proudly in their rooms. It made Parker's Legos, photos, signed baseballs, trophies, medals, football helmets, cheap souvenirs, and snow globes not just relatable but as if they were an integral part of who I was. Dana hadn't lost somebody else's precious child; she'd lost Will or Matthew. It was like putting in new contact lenses for the first time, seeing everything more clearly—only somebody punched you in the stomach at the same time.

I couldn't feel what Dana felt, and I desperately didn't want to. But that didn't mean it didn't scare the shit out of me—and make me want to hug her for a thousand years.

Returning to the living room, a warm, inviting, and beautiful space, we each drank a mimosa. After a few precious moments of chatting and laughing, Dana said we would take a tour of her neighborhood on her golf cart. It would end at their clubhouse, where we would eat lunch. Following her out the back door, I grabbed my purse.

"What do you need that for?" Dana asked.

"So I can pay for my lunch," I replied.

"That's hilarious, Constant," she replied, laughing loudly. "Your money is no good here."

As Dana drove us through her neighborhood on the cool, crisp, perfect day that felt to me, from the frozen tundra of Ohio, like early fall, I took in the Southern charm surrounding me. Every home was expertly manicured and decorated beautifully for the holidays. The driveway entrance to the club featured a giant replica of the Arc de Triomphe in Paris, and the clubhouse itself looked more like a luxurious French château than a golf destination in South Louisiana.

As I followed Dana up the stairs into the front entrance of

the club, she turned to me and smiled. "Listen," she said, "this might be a bigger deal than what I said."

I smiled back, wondering, *What could she possibly mean?*

Making our way down a corridor into the restaurant, which had huge windows overlooking a pond and the golf course, we took a left into a secondary room. And there it was—the bigger deal.

At a huge, rectangular dining room table sat what must have been a dozen of Dana's friends on each side, including her best friend, Angela, and three of her four daughters, Alli, Mady, and Peyton. I had met most of the attendees in Memphis and was introduced to the ones I didn't know. Everyone hugged me and welcomed me.

This was our "little lunch."

Rounding the table to the seat of honor at the far end, I sat down, and Dana took her place to my right. Looking down at my plate, I saw a special menu featuring five or six lunch options. At the top of the glossy card, it said #CONSTANTLUNCHEON, and at the bottom, WELCOME, AMY! with a picture of the arc we had just driven past.

Holy crap. I was in Louisiana, at Dana Dugas Rivera's country club, at a special "luncheon" for me. I just couldn't get my head around it. It was like standing in the ocean, feeling gentle waves roll by repeatedly, only to have a gigantic swell of salt water come out of nowhere and overwhelm me. The swell of emotion took me out. I may even have lost my bathing suit.

Even though I was well and truly in a state of shock and awe, I got that this was a historic moment. And so I did what any other person in 2016 would do: I took out my iPhone and covertly snapped a few photos.

As I did so, I looked down at the surface of the table and noticed something that looked oddly familiar. Yes—it looked like the card I had bought Dana at a little shop outside San Diego on my trip to California the previous spring break. When I looked down the long expanse of the table, I saw that it was "decorated" with what looked like *all* of the cards I had sent her, along with many of the typewritten PFYP cards.

Oh. My. God.

I turned to Dana and said, motioning toward the long table in front of us, "It's all the letters. . . . I can't believe it's all the letters. You kept them."

"Yeah," she replied, laughing. "What did you think I did, throw them all away?"

While I didn't think she had thrown them away, and though she had expressed her gratitude for my #CONSTANT contact, somehow I had still been under the impression that the letters were an unnecessary sideshow. At best, I hoped, they were a distraction. But now they were a table decoration at an event where I was the honoree.

We ordered our food and drinks, Dana quietly checking in with me on each decision, both of us selecting the same items from the menu. It was as if, once again, she had an inherent sense that I, a stranger in a strange land, needed reassurance, although we exchanged very few words.

I did attempt to thank Dana and tell her how grateful and moved I was. I don't even know what I said to her, but I'm sure it was totally inadequate.

After we had eaten, she stood up and publicly gave me two gifts, both tagged #CONSTANT." The first was a Louisiana-themed T-shirt that said, "You Are My Sunshine," and the second was a box of chocolates—which she pointed out she had regifted from one of her students. Just like in her letters, she was honest, generous, and hilarious, all in one breath.

As the attendees resumed chatting, I got up silently and

found my way to the restroom. I was still being medicated for the aftermath of my Lyme disease and had taken my medicine before leaving Dana's house for the club. The drinks and my state of overwhelm put my stomach into a precarious situation. I went into one of the stalls and threw up. I also prayed. As good as I felt about everything that had gone down thus far, I wasn't sure how I was supposed to act, or leave, or do anything.

As I was washing my hands, Mady came in and found me. I'm not sure how long I had been gone, but I'm guessing it was beyond what a reasonable bathroom break would have taken.

"Come on, Constant," she said. "Mom wants you back out there."

"Okay," I agreed, following her. "This is pretty incredible."

"You deserve it all and more," she responded, smiling.

As the lunch wrapped up, Dana invited everyone to come back to her house to extend the visit. Those who could do so agreed to meet us there, while those who couldn't hugged Dana and then me.

"We all love you," one friend said, holding on tightly.

"Thanks for what you've done for Dana," another emoted, looking me straight in the eye, with tears running down her face.

When lunch was over, we jumped back on the cart and rode back to the Riveras'. Gathered in Dana's kitchen, we laughed about the shared experience of the holidays—the in-laws, the outlaws, the stress, the joy. It was almost like I was back in Ohio, having the same honest discourse with my own circle of close friends. As much of a stranger as I was to this group in Louisiana, I almost felt as if, even at this early date, they were my people. Like I was just falling back into this part of my life, which had always been there waiting for me.

We also discussed how the holidays looked drastically different for the Riveras. It was a truth that wasn't so much hidden but perhaps more difficult to keep in mind as we stood near Dana's perfectly decorated Christmas tree. What we could see looked festive, while what we couldn't was not.

"It's going to suck, and I just want it to be over," Dana told us.

No one said much in response to this comment, I'm assuming her people simply got that there were no words. What they did offer was support and comfort, subtly and nonverbally.

Angela nodded silently, as a tear slowly descended her cheek. Laurie and Cheryl, friends I had met in Memphis, each put a hand on Dana, while Andria, someone I had met only that day, offered her a tissue.

As the sun started to set, I told Dana that I needed to go. It was the day before Christmas Eve, and a Friday, so I assumed the traffic on Interstate 10 was going to be heavy. It was after five o'clock, and it would likely take me five hours to get back to my family's place.

Dana walked me out to my car, giving us a few precious moments to talk one-on-one. I had hoped for a time like this. While I didn't have a lot I wanted to say, seeing her individually, in person, meant that I could try to express something that I hadn't ever been able to do in the letters.

"Look, Dana," I said, "there are a couple things I need to tell you. First, I have a message to deliver to you: God loves you and your family. It's the only reason I'm standing here in your driveway in Lafayette, Louisiana. Next," I continued, "there's something I want to say that I've never been able to write about; I just couldn't bring myself to do it. Though I one hundred percent believe what I've been telling you, that God's love for you and your family is the reason for our connection, as a mom, I know there's a part of it I'll never, ever get. While I'll never stop praying for it, you gotta know the reality of a 'path to peace' seems ridiculous, considering what you've lost. I'll continue to pray for it, and I completely trust God, but I personally don't get it. I just need you to know that for all I don't know, and all I don't get, *I know that.*"

She didn't respond verbally but shook her head vigorously in agreement. Then she hugged me tight.

"My girls . . ." she said, with tears running down her face. "They have started talking about how one day you'll stop writing the letters."

"I don't know," I responded. "I don't have any plans to stop, but if I do, I guess I'll know when to, just like when I started writing them in the first place."

Again, she nodded. "You better get on the road," she said after another hug. "This summer you'll come and sleep for a couple of nights."

"Absolutely," I agreed.

Just as it had in Memphis, walking away felt like ripping myself from something that I wasn't supposed to leave behind.

I got only about ten miles from Dana's neighborhood before I had to pull off the road. I broke down, sobbing uncontrollably, asking and, perhaps even more so, demanding that God himself explain it to me: "Why?" Why had this happened to Jim and Dana and their girls and not to "other" people? *Nobody* deserved this crap, but why did *her* heart have to be broken in a way that seemed beyond repair?

The Riveras were generous and kind and accepting and loving. Why them?

I knew there wasn't an answer to that question.

As far as framing it as "God's will" and accepting it as such went, that was much easier to do if you lived in a vacuum that didn't include someone you loved suffering, both visibly and invisibly, to a degree that you could never fathom.

If I—several critical steps back from the horrors of ground zero—couldn't find a lesson of acceptance in it, how would Dana, Jim, and their girls ever do so?

It meant perhaps living the rest of their lives with no answer.

It made me want to rip the steering wheel off its base and beat something with it.

I pulled back onto the road and eventually stopped crying. As I listened to music and talked to God, a sense of what felt almost like invincibility crept over me. Despite the fact that all the "amazing" things that were happening all around me hinged on the Riveras' tragedy—something that would *never* be "right" for me—I felt an undeniable and unexpected wave of hope. It didn't fit the circumstances, but it was there.

If the #CONSTANT luncheon in Lafayette, Louisiana, had just happened, then anything could. If I could blindly write all of those freaking letters, sharing all of my many feelings, with no expectations, and then—boom—see them all laid out in front of me, surrounded on every side by strangers who knew my name and valued me, then anything, and I mean anything, truly *was* possible.

In the same way that no one could ever have predicted Dana's and my story, none of us can predict our own future, either. While we cannot possibly know what lies just ahead, hope is justifiable. Not only do stories such as the ones detailed here provide concrete evidence that there *is* something to look forward to, but here in the present, we have no proof to the contrary.

Letter #464

⁑

I didn't pick back up where I had left off, in late November, with the Facebook project until after New Year's. A journal entry from early January explains the delay and sets the stage for the final leg of my quest to finish.

January 2, 2017

Well, I took the entire month of December off. I certainly didn't plan to, but I did. Maybe it was for the best—I think it was Memphis/St. Jude/the holidays/Lafayette/ the #CONSTANT luncheon, etc., behind the pause. So, one part busy plus three parts emotional state.

I'm not sure I want to continue on—but I know I have to finish. No question there. I will say that the holidays brought lots of FB reaction—in person/in Xmas cards/in writing—and I'm going to list all of that here.

Next, there was that one time Dana laid out ALL of my cards/letters/PFYPs on the table (literally) at the #CONSTANT luncheon. Let's just say that's some SUPER POWERFUL business. I don't know that anything bigger has ever happened in my emotional life.

Okay, so, here we go. First, I will attempt to track responses/adds from the end of November through December. Next, I'll put November–December stats into a separate journal. Then I'll start the letters again, beginning with January 2, 2017.

Ultimately, I don't feel "guilty" about this thirty-day

delay, as it will likely make the finish line easier to reach.

New goal: my forty-ninth birthday! April 25, 2017.

Letter #464 was to a musician who had taught me private saxophone lessons from sixth to eighth grade. I was in the band from middle school through high school, and she laid the foundation for my participation.

I am not a musically gifted person. First, I lack a sense of basic rhythm, and beyond that, I'm not physically coordinated. Number 464 worked hard to help me overcome some of these deficiencies. She was successful enough that while I wasn't ever going to make a career out of playing the alto saxophone, I was going to not only enjoy band but be where I needed to be to meet "my people."

Number 464 and I also had a similar sense of humor and zest for life. I believed she groomed my personality by encouraging me—an early teen—to be myself as much as she did my musical skills.

January 7, 2017

It's amazing to me—almost jaw-dropping—that life hooked us up so early on. You were a young private-lesson teacher, and I was a lost middle-school student with a bowl cut and zero musical talent. But even then, we were kindred spirits! It was totally meant to be, and I'm sincerely thankful.

THANK YOU for being one of my life's best and most influential mentors, despite the fact I was not a good saxophone player (the fact that I even reached the "decent" level was a credit to your abilities as a teacher). You gave me such confidence by celebrating my

personality and supporting me, and the fun and
shenanigans we shared gave me an example of how to
deal with life and relationships. It's important to
remember that you were the leader—teaching hard work
and fun and instilling self-confidence in a girl who had
little—and I got to follow you by example.

Look at my FB page and look at my life—your
fingerprints are all over it. It's also hilarious that we both
have Facebook profile pictures featuring selfies with bad
hair/wigs. . . . Thanks for teaching me private and life
lessons!

While #464 didn't respond directly to me, she did comment on a post regarding the Facebook project as it was nearing completion.

April 20, 2017

As a recipient of a cherished letter, all I can say is WOW! I have been meaning to sit down and write you back, but it seems like I just haven't gotten to it, so the sheer volume of letters you have written makes me feel very inadequate! And very impressed!

While my exchange with #464 was yet another example of how the Facebook project gave me the opportunity to say thank you, it also highlighted a deeper point. Without the forced act of figuring out what to say about each recipient, I would never have understood how important friends' contributions were to my life story. This was especially true of people like #464, who were a part of my earlier life, or who played an active role briefly. While I may have understood that these individuals were key to who I would become, I hadn't ever sat down and really considered how real and lasting their impact was.

Now, I understand how, at any point in our lives, we can interact with people who can change us fundamentally. It's true whether our paths cross for just a few months or for several years, whether we meet them when we're fifteen or fifty-five. The key is to remain teachable, even as we mature, age, and experience life. If we keep our eyes and minds open, every individual we meet has the potential to teach us something of great value.

Letter #475

Letter #475 was to an individual whom I had worked in the same department with during my time in the adult-beverage industry in the late 1990s and early 2000s. Like many people who work together closely, we had formed a bond that can be achieved only by slogging through the everyday landscape of employment. We had definitely "toiled" together.

Eventually, I was promoted within our section of the company and ultimately became #475's direct supervisor. This led to the unfortunate circumstance that I, at the direction of my higher-ups, had to let her go.

February 6, 2017

So, there are several things I want to say to you, and I am really excited for this opportunity:

1) Back in the day, at work, that was a mess. I want to acknowledge that the management team there (which included me) wasn't always right, and that personally you were a good friend to me and my family. I so enjoyed spending those years with you and the rest of the team.

2) I'm glad for FB—in your case, because I still get to experience your hilarity and passionate personality. Without FB, it wouldn't be possible to "keep in touch." Please know that I still enjoy being your friend, even if only virtually.

3) You've had major health issues. For that, I am sorry. I hope (and this is how it seems via FB) that you really are doing better. I also appreciate your posting about some of your challenges, as that gives the rest of us, including me, the opportunity to pray and be concerned.

4) This is REAL life, so the bigger, not-on-FB story is, it can be difficult, wonderful, scary, awesome, unsettling, unbelievable, lonely, and the best thing ever—all at the same time. I very sincerely hope that your version of real life—and that of your people—is more joy-filled than hard.

Due to the unusual and fraught circumstances surrounding my final in-person encounter with #475, I was especially delighted to receive a Facebook message from her three weeks after I wrote her.

February 28, 2017

I got your letter yesterday. It was the nicest heartfelt letter I have ever gotten. I am personally a huge fan of Facebook because it allows me to stay connected with friends and family and share photos. I value your friendship and hope we can remain friends to the end. . . . Thank you again for such a wonderful letter. Luv ya!

I had spent fifteen years feeling guilty about terminating #475's employment. Yes, I was doing my job, but as a fellow human being, and in this case a friend, I understood that my actions had many implications.

Then, because of some ridiculous quest to find meaning in the culture of social media, I wrote her a meaningful letter. And she wrote me back. And told me she wanted to be friends forever. And that she loved me.

We can never know what will happen if we scrape up the courage to reach out to someone who we assume might have a grudge against us. Trying to make things right liberates us from fear. It's one less person we're afraid of running into in the grocery store.

While we can't change what we did, we can clean the slate.

Letter #492

The recipient of letter #492 was a guy whom I had known over many years at camp. He and both of his siblings had attended Olympia as campers and counselors at the same time I had. Though they were a few years younger than I was, our lives had intersected repeatedly. Most recently, #492 and I had reconnected at a camp reunion.

I was also friends, on Facebook and in real life, with #492's brother, who, like Willie and I, had met someone at camp and then started a life with that person. Unlike our version of the Camp Olympia dream, #492's brother and bride doubled up and went on to have four children together. By 2016, the oldest of these offspring was approximately seven and the youngest was two. Tragically, on January 30, 2017, the young mother of four died suddenly. She was only thirty-four.

When I drew #492's name out of the box, just seventeen days after his sister-in-law passed away, I literally gasped. Though I was well aware of what had happened, I hadn't yet reached out to any of the family. I had been planning on waiting until the "casseroles stopped coming." But somebody, or something else, had obviously decided I needed to say something sooner.

February 16, 2017

First, let me offer my very sincere condolences to you and your people. Your sister-in-law's passing is heartbreaking to all of us—your Olympia family. That said, I can't imagine the pain you and yours are personally suffering. For that, I am gut-wrenchingly sorry.

The way this process works is, I draw a name out of a box of all my FB friends' names each day and write that person, no matter what (i.e., no matter how awkward— as in, "Hello, sixth-grade-band friend"). This makes the timing of your letter seem almost meant to be.

So, again, since I have the chance, I want you to know how heartbroken I am for you and your brother and your family. And I want you to know that I'll be praying—not just in the next couple of weeks, but for as long as possible. Here's the thing: I'm a prayer person—it's how I roll. So, seriously, sincerely, legitimately, you and your people are covered.

I realize my words are inadequate, but the sentiments are totally real.

While #492 didn't respond directly to my letter, he did comment on a Facebook post on my birthday in April of that same year.

April 25, 2017

Happy birthday, Amy! Thank you so much for the letter. It meant a lot.

I was just pulling names out of a box, a random act that, log-ically speaking, couldn't be manipulated by anything other than pure chance. So why had timing been such a recurring theme— both for me and for the recipients of the letters—during the Facebook project? Why had I pulled out an old friend's name four months before his death and had a chance to reconnect with him one final time? Why had I pulled out my cousin's wife's name on the first anniversary of her mother's death? And why had #492's name come out less than three weeks after his thirty-four-year-old sister-in-law suddenly died?

Maybe, just maybe, there really is no such thing as a coincidence. Maybe, just maybe, something we can't see is directing all the things we can see.

Letter #500

Letter #500 meant one thing—I was fewer than one hundred letters from the end, and *I was going to finish*. For all the thousands of moments where I thought I couldn't write another word and was sure I would never reach my goal, this was the moment that I finally believed.

The five hundred–letter plateau also marked the beginning of my being totally in awe of the number of people I'd actually written a letter to. I can vividly remember sitting at my desk and thinking, *Holy crap, you've written five hundred freaking letters*. It was a place that I hadn't really let myself go to previously, even when other people brought it up, because I was always so focused on moving ahead—trudging forward to a finish line that I didn't even believe in. It was back to some sort of destiny that manifested itself in a gut instinct that I could neither explain nor deny.

The recipient of Letter #500 was the wife of one of Willie's dearest friends from college. While she and I weren't close, I had been at her wedding and in her home on several occasions, and we had many mutual friends. She also had a big personality, just like I did.

February 24, 2017

Well, after a year and a half of writing, I can confidently say I will NEVER be the same again. What's changed the most is my own heart—which has been transformed through the process of realizing I have been gifted with five hundred–plus unique individuals—all a part of my life story. Some I have nothing in common with; some I agree with wholeheartedly. The connecting factor is that they ALL illustrate that God's hand has been all up in my business since the very beginning of my life. They are all LOVE—regardless of whether they share my beliefs and views or not.

You are letter #500—an unbelievable benchmark that means I have fewer than one hundred letters to write to actually complete an endeavor that I've believed so many times was unachievable. It's pretty amazing what people have been planted at #100, #200, #300, #400.... They're all like you—individually spectacular.

I never received a reply from #500, but that didn't take away from the fact that it was one of the biggest achievements of my entire life. I didn't need anyone to validate that; the new, improved version of my own heart was all the confirmation I would ever need.

February 2017

*R*ight around this same time, I heard from Dana again. It was the first letter I received from her after the intense in-person time we shared in both Memphis and at the #CONSTANT luncheon.

> *Anyway, we spent January the 4th ☹ here at home with friends and family. We cooked, played a game, drank . . . I was glad it was over. It just seems that the pain deepens as time goes by. And I don't know how that's possible, but it is. I want to see his seventeen-year-old self, kiss his cheek, fuss at him for leaving the towel on the ground. . . . I still wake up and go to bed shocked that he's not here.*

> *Two weeks ago, all four girls and their SO's came home for the weekend. It was really awesome. Amy slept over; we had five couples over on Saturday with their kids #thatshowweroll #kidsalwaysincluded. It was a full-on pool-playing, music-playing, beverage-drinking party! And then I woke up Sunday with a pit in my stomach and a hurt heart and started crying. The kids would be leaving (which has always made me sad even precancer). Parker was still not there (he LOVED and ADORED when everyone was home). The reality of where we are*

overwhelms me at times—lots of times, actually—almost daily.

The day and then week proceeded to get worse, Jim and I weren't getting along (we usually do, but we occasionally get mad at each other just to have someone to be mad at —though we do recognize this for what it is), and my heart just hurt for about nine solid days, twenty-four hours a day.

The honest truth is, I think I've liked, in a very sad way, really being in a prolonged funk. It almost helps me to deal with reality. Crazy—I know others feel this way, but I avoid commiserating, as others' stories make me even sadder.

Only after reuniting with Dana in the flesh could I gain a better perspective on how the person who wrote me letters was, on many levels, different than the physical manifestation of the individual I had now spent time with. What I had seen on the outside—an outgoing, appreciative woman who wanted everyone around her to be happy and have fun—was a sharp contrast with the one who shared her devastating internal reality in the letters. Despite all the laughter and fun that connected us, at every turn I was reminded that Dana was still hurting profoundly.

Then there were her surprising revelations about how her grief wove itself through her everyday life. I would never have thought about how hard Sundays might be for someone who had suffered an incomprehensible loss. I also would have assumed, I suppose, that being around others who had dealt with a similar anguish would provide comfort, instead of making things worse. Additionally, it seemed counterintuitive to think that being in a "prolonged funk" was something that could be good for somebody, especially her.

What I've continued to learn from Dana—repeatedly—is that there are no assumptions or right answers where grief is concerned. Each person approaches it differently, and therefore not only do they require individual care, they cope with it in their own way.

While no human is adequately equipped to respond to someone's unique despair, no matter how badly we want to, there are things we *can* do. We can avoid assuming anything, we can listen attentively, we can be present, we can know that a smile doesn't always equal happiness, and we can love the crap out of one another. And we can do these things without stopping, all the while being aware that none of it will ever be enough.

Letter #509

Letter #509 was to a camp friend whom I had known since my teens. When I first met him, I was a camper and he was a fixture on the summer staff. Eventually, we worked together at what was the end of his time as a counselor and the beginning of mine. I had always looked up to him, as he was one of the "cool" people who was not only older than I but well liked. The friend group I was in all aspired to be #509 when we grew up.

He was also one of those inclusive individuals who seem to have an inherent talent for seeing people on the outskirts who might need encouragement to join in. I can remember the first "counselor appreciation" night I ever attended. We were at a local pizza parlor, and I was looking for a place to sit down. Most everyone attending was older than I was, and I felt hesitant about where I was supposed to go. Number 509 was sitting at a long table with a dozen or so of the "it" people at camp that term. If it had been Hollywood, they would all have been considered A-listers.

"Come sit with us, Amy!" #509 exclaimed, coming across as sincere.

"Yeah, right here," another attendee offered, moving a chair from another table to squeeze me in.

That small gesture got me off on the right foot as a counselor. It wasn't so much that I got introduced to the "right" people; it was that I believed that I belonged with them.

From what I remembered, #509 had settled in the Dallas area and did something in construction. That was all I knew.

March 1, 2017

In preparing to write this letter, I spent some time really looking at your profile page. This kind of light stalking is probably one of the best things to come out of this ridiculous project—I've taken the time to really consider each of these relationships as actual individuals, as opposed to news feed blips. For you, I had no idea that you were recently widowed. For that, I am sincerely and deeply sorry. I can't even imagine what you are suffering—nor would I pretend to—but please know that I will honestly pray for you and your two boys. It makes me realize that as much as FB keeps us in touch, it does not.

I didn't receive a reply from #509 until much later in the year. His handwritten letter was on monogrammed stationery that he lovingly indicated was his mother's.

November 30, 2017

Amy,

I recently read a letter from you dated March 1, 2017. It was sent to my work office and never quite made it to me until this month. We recently moved offices; maybe that was the primary reason.

I certainly am not a social media hound; I actually prefer phone conversations, and texting is convenient too. But I will basically stop what I'm doing if a Camp O friend needs help, encouragement, support, etc.

My wife passed away in 2015 of nonsmoking lung cancer. She was as fit as a fitness trainer—no idea how she got cancer. Two and a half months was all it took from the day we found out.

My mother passed away last year, two weeks before my brother-in-law. Then my father, brother, and sister were diagnosed with cancer in 2015–'16. Terrible last eighteen months, to say the least. So my two teenage boys and I are trying to make the best of it.

Thank you for your wonderful comments.

Though I had found out about #509's wife's passing when I was preparing to write his letter, I had no idea about the other challenges he, my old friend who had been so kind to me, was facing.

This "if you only knew" theme was another ongoing thread in the project. The assertion that we can't really know the reality of any of our friends' situations isn't limited to those lives that look perfect in comparison with our own. It also applies to those individuals who don't post often and who don't share.

It's a reminder to treat people delicately even when they don't seem delicate. To approach other people with the same sensitivity and care that we want to be handled with.

Letter #515

The recipient of letter #515 was one of the best friends of Mady Rivera, Dana and Jim's third daughter. We had met at the marathon weekend in Memphis and, despite our age gap, had hit it off. We had danced together, cracked each other up, and made what was another uncharted but meaningful connection.

We became Facebook official in December 2016.

March 4, 2017

A few things:

1) THANK YOU for being my FB friend. Though I'm guessing you already get that I put out a cool, stylish, almost amazing vibe online, being friends with a happening twentysomething from Lafayette does nothing but enhance my budding reputation. Though I get how this must work the other way (i.e., what it must do for YOUR online status to be connected to a forty-five-plus-er with a minivan in Ohio), really, I assure you, there is NO reason to gush. #weareonthesamepage

2) Given that we're only, like, seven years apart (my calculator is broken, so that's an estimate), we should probably make it a point to hang out—have a few strong-ish beverages and talk about our feelings. I have a propensity to pick up guys—really attractive ones who have actual employment opportunities—so place selection will be key.

3) And here's the actual deal: Given that I pray for our Rivera connection every day, I pray for your BFF Mady

—you guessed it—every day. Despite my love of shenanigans, the praying situation is one of the REALEST deals in my life. And I get how BFF-ing works —you and Mady are there for each other, carry each other's burdens, freak out accordingly, and basically "do life" together. So, in a very concrete and real way, YOU are an answer to MY prayers for Mady. THIS IS HUGE.

While I didn't hear back from #515 directly, she did post on Facebook, sharing a newspaper article about Dana, me, and both letter-writing campaigns that was published the month after I wrote to her.

April 15, 2017

Truly a special woman with a heart of gold who radiates love for each and every person she meets! Beyond thankful to know you and the way God works through you in every letter sent, times we've #chilled, and hashtags you've created. You are loved and appreciated more than you'll ever know and have a special gift! #CONSTANT

The connections between Dana's and my people were not only multiplying but deepening. Number 515 was someone I had met only twice, very briefly, but we were linked by something much bigger. Yes, we had a similar sense of humor, but what bound us was profound. It couldn't be properly explained, not because there were no words, but because we here in the physical world couldn't fully grasp it.

Technology is a marvelous thing, affording us opportunities and experiences that our ancestors couldn't have dreamed of. But it also makes us confident, sure that we have tamed the world. However, what we can see and put our hands on is just one layer of reality.

Where our forefathers and foremothers were more in touch with the reality of life's mysteries, we are more hesitant to accept the presence of the unknown. Ironically, people from the past are often viewed as gullible naïfs, believing in myths that we, the haughty futurists, have debunked.

What we've sacrificed in the name of concrete advancement is the belief that there is so much more than what we can see, than what can be proven. Just because we can't explain something and account for its rock-solid realness doesn't mean that it isn't 100 percent, grade-A truth.

Letter #533

Letter #533 was to Jim and Dana's second daughter, Lauren. At this point, just fifty Facebook letters shy of the finish line, not only had I gained tremendous perspective, I had lost much of the hesitation I had felt earlier in the project. That affected how I approached the letters I wrote to the other Rivera girls; Peyton came first (in April 2016), Mady was next (in July 2016), and Alli was after that (in January 2017).

March 16, 2017

Greetings and salutations! Well, that glorious day has finally arrived when I pull your name out of my box of many letter-writing options. For me, it's an exciting thing because I contend (still and always) that the entire reason for this campaign is God's love (#therealdeal) for you and your family. Somehow, in my writing to your mom, God's "Rivera love" spilled over into wild idea #2 (okay, really it's more like absurd idea #3,722, if we're counting everything from all of my thirty-six years) to write all of my FB people a letter.

It's God's Rivera love in every envelope, despite what any recipient does/doesn't believe, their politics, their situation, etc. And it all started with God overtaking my heart with you and your people. Pure craziness? Abso-freaking-lutely! But totally, 100 percent true? You betcha! #srsly

I'm super glad we're connected on social media and in real life. I mean that very sincerely. Meeting you and your people in Memphis was an honor for me, Willie, and Matthew. THANK YOU for welcoming us so wonderfully after we—okay, I—inserted myself into your lives. I've told your mom this, but I think one of the most compelling parts of our story is not me rapid-firing words at y'all but instead your family's response. From Dana's writing back in the first place to the Daughters family's inclusion in your world, it's all about the way we've been received. To me, it says so much about why God wants us connected in the first place—the Riveras are some SPECIAL people. #forrealz

I can't tell you much about religion or even explain what is really going on with our families unique connection, but I am sure of one thing. In fact, I've never been surer of anything: GOD LOVES THE RIVERA FAMILY, AND GOD LOVES LAUREN RIVERA. He loves you so much that I'm not going to shut up. Honestly, if I was looking from the outside in, this would all seem unbelievable, but from the perspective of my own heart, it's the realest thing I know.

Lauren responded to my letter via Facebook messenger about a month after I wrote her.

April 20, 2017

You are the sweetest human, and you are making my day!!! Got your letter from my mama about two weeks ago and cried as I read your sweet and perfect words! What an amazing journey and experience we have gotten to be a part of through you. When are you coming to visit? We miss our friend!

When I set out to try to write all of my Facebook friends in July 2015, only months into writing Dana, I could never have imagined that I'd wind up sending a handwritten letter to each of her and Jim's four daughters. That I'd meet them in person. That I'd consider them real-life friends and they'd count me as the same. Letter #533 illustrates how the Facebook project ultimately intersected, beautifully and in a life-changing way, with the Dear Dana letters.

It also brings up a key yet underplayed element of the story. Namely, my acknowledgment to #533, Lauren Rivera, that the incredible sequence of events that followed my reconnection with Dana and Jim would not have happened without their being who they are.

Human nature dictates that without a response from the Riveras, I would have stopped writing them at some point. It's no coincidence that my "big idea" to write all my Facebook friends a letter came just ninety days after Dana's first letter to me.

None of what happened next—the Facebook letters, the PFYPs, Memphis, the run, hearts being blown up across the globe—would have occurred if Dana, despite the fact that she was living through hell, had not responded to me; if Jim and the girls, despite their suffering the same reality, had not supported the entire affair; and if they had not welcomed my people and me so seamlessly into their lives.

Though I have and will likely continue to receive lots of kudos for writing the letters, none of what this book details would have happened if Dana hadn't written me back.

What if the best parts of our life have nothing to do with something *we* did? What if both of my letter-writing campaigns were so impactful because I *wasn't* in control of them?

Regardless of what each of us might identify as a "higher

power" in our own experience, many times the stories concocted by this force (God, fate, etc.) are better than the ones we'd write for ourselves.

Letter #535

Letter #535 was to one of my dearest friends. He and his wife—also one of my BFFs—were part of the group that moved from Texas to Ohio at the same time. Number 535 and I share a love for random knowledge, college football, and golf. I also deeply respected and admired him.

I wrote him just a few months before he and his wife, Willie and I, and two other couples were due to take a boat trip together. The trip had been a lifelong dream for #535, who had been meticulously planning our voyage for several years. Originally, we were supposed to embark in 2015, but #535 put the entire trip on hold until I had fully recovered from my Lyme disease and Rocky Mountain spotted fever.

We can only hope to have one friend like this come along in a lifetime.

March 17, 2017

You are letter #535, so I'm literally just forty-five or so letters from ACTUALLY finishing. Honestly, I don't know if I ever expected to complete the list. As I told you and Shonda at dinner, this project has changed the way I look at EVERYTHING. Suddenly I feel less inclined to hate (maybe a strong word—perhaps "dislike") others based on our differences. Also, I realize I've assumed a lot of things about people, only to be proven wrong over and over again by their heartfelt, revealing replies. I'm also less inclined to compare myself and my situation with others. I had no idea what kind of impact the letters would have on me personally.

*To you, I would like to say a few things. A lot of this is
going to be either borderline or full-on cheesy, so I
recommend you brace yourself and take it like a man.
Also, if you never want to speak of it again (outside of
both of us being smashed on a boat) that's good with me.
#seriously*

I received a handwritten reply from #535 less than two
weeks after I wrote him.

March 30, 2017

*I also think it's great you have single-handedly started a
campaign to save the US post office! A lot of mail carriers
are grateful!*

*Finding something to say to all of your Facebook friends is
a real testament to the great writer you are—and I'm
sure just like my and Shonda's letters, they have touched
them beyond what you can imagine.*

For me, any good the letters did or were yet to do would always be a credit to my reconnection with the Riveras and the
limitless power of unconditional love (which for me means
God's love). That said, I accepted that my name was on every
letter and that therefore some level of acknowledgment was going to be attached to me.

Regardless of what the driving force behind it was, I do
know that no matter how many years pass and how many times I
attempt to gain true perspective on it, I'll never fully understand
the depth of the impact of the Facebook project.

It's a commonality across human interaction. We simply
cannot ever know the effect, positive or negative, that we have

on another individual. We will get glimpses, and occasionally we'll be blown away by the way someone responds to something we did, but other than that, it's like a blind march forward into an unknown that we hope is fruitful.

The key is not to stop listening to that little voice in our heads. To continue to press on boldly, in those ways that feel completely right, regardless of any lack of feedback. Maybe changing the world is all about not expecting to but never, ever giving up on trying to.

23

March 2017

*O*n late March, I received another letter from Dana.

This week was rough—each night working in Parker's room, setting it up (BTW, it is absolutely adorable and he has told me he loves it!), Jim and I both in there, arguing over this or that, both understanding it wasn't really about us or the argument . . . It was just HARD!

Saturday we went through his clothes. Sweet Monica, my neighbor, had boxed them up beautifully a few months ago and delivered them back to me on Friday. We also found his book sack, still packed, and there was a journal from English. Mady would read it as we worked, and it was like he was here with us. We could hear him, we laughed, we cried . . . Anyway, by noon we were done, and Lauren, Alli, and Amy left, and I just lost it! I cried and just wanted his room back to how it was! Anyway, crying like that does help emotionally, but man, it wears me out.

One thing impacted me deeply from your last letter. You said that Parker's ongoing relationship with Jesus has so much to do with our connection. Those words, in particular "ongoing," were profound for me. I do think about his "ongoing" relationship with Jesus, and it gives me hope. I also get baffled by "our connection," even as it has become such a big part of my life. I'm still in awe of it.

You have become a part of us. Beyond what you've done for me, what you have "shown" my girls is something more valuable than words can convey. They have witnessed a rare occurrence through you, and it has been very meaningful for them.

She wrapped up with this:

Well, as I close, this paper is from Parker's school notebook. I adore looking at his messy handwriting. I actually had flashbacks last week of him crying because he was in pain. It made me so sad and then comforted that he has no more suffering. That said, I am still in shock that he's not here. I pretend he's at school. . . . Anyway, these letters are almost a journal for me.

While that was the end of the letter, there was another page. As I flipped it over to look at it, I gasped. It was Parker's class notes on India in his messy handwriting. Underneath his writing, Dana wrote:

This was the next page after the last page in your letter— he obviously skipped pages. Hope it's not weird that I included it, but really, I am a strange bird, so who cares?

All there was left to do was cry.

I cried at seeing the visceral reminder of Parker. I cried at holding something in my hands that he had held in his. I cried about my own sons. I cried because I was scared. I cried because every word I had written was inadequate. Most of all, I cried for Dana. Despite all the flowery prose and the true goodness that our relationship exuded, her grief would never end in this lifetime.

Letter #542

Though I had met #542 in person, it had been only a couple of times that occurred over a four-day cruise my brother, sister, and I had taken for my sister's fiftieth birthday in June 2016. The entire basis of my "relationship" with #542 was a series of fun evenings in the ship's piano bar. After I met her initially, late the first night of the cruise, she and her cousin and my siblings and I agreed to hook up each night for the remainder of our voyage.

March 20, 2017

In fact, you are my ONLY Carnival Cruise Facebook friend. We met only briefly—the real basis of our in-person connection was a few hilarious, ridiculous, fun hours in the piano bar, on a ship, each with some of our life's besties alongside us. We were both pausing from our "regular lives" when our paths intersected, and even though there was A LOT of shenanigans and singing and laughing, we also managed enough of a real conversation for me to glean that we are both BFFs with Jesus.

It's also amazing that we met just after our oldest graduated from high school and was standing at the jump-off point to his freshman year of college. Fast-forward nine months, and you are prepping for YOUR son's graduation and for sending him off to UT. I sincerely feel for you, friend. I look forward to the rejoicing and hope your heart is ready for the bittersweet, long goodbye —which is really more of a "see you in three weeks"—that is scary, exhilarating, and pride-filled all in the same sob.

*I hope you post pics—to me, they will serve as a reminder
to pray for your heart.*

*You are such a special part of the memories we share from
Kim's fiftieth-birthday cruise. I hope we meet again.
Until then, I wish you joy, love, and most of all peace!*

Though #542 didn't reply directly to my letter, she did post
on my Facebook page on my birthday.

April 25, 2017

Happy birthday, Amy! What began as a fun chance encounter
at the cruise ship piano bar has led me to discover (on FB) a
wonderful, kind, selfless person who inspires so many. I hope
you enjoy your day.

Letter #542 is a reminder that we can make a meaningful
connection anywhere. That includes but is not limited to the
middle of the Gulf of Mexico while a pianist bangs out the
chorus to Def Leppard and Neil Diamond songs. And while its
impact can be muted by a culture that holds the acquisition of
material things in high esteem, one of the most valuable assets
in life is making a genuine connection with another human
being. The newness never wears off a heart that glows with the
warmth of friendship.

Letter #547

The recipient of Letter #547 was my husband's uncle, technically my uncle-in-law, a salty yet sweet former game warden. Even though he and his family all lived in the northwestern corner of the United States, where my father-in-law grew up, I had physically interacted with and therefore gotten to know him on several occasions.

He is opinionated, honest, wise, funny, and a true outdoorsman. My favorite story of him is one that my husband's cousins tell with great fondness and humor. They—two sisters—were raised in Hawaii and California in a suburban setting. Uncle Chuck, who lived in a remote setting outside Portland, Oregon, lived off the land. On one visit, the girls and their mom sat on the couch in the living room, chatting with Aunt Betty. Uncle Chuck burst into the room with a deer he had recently felled. After laying a sheet of plastic on the shag carpet, he proceeded to dress the animal as the girls looked on with eyes wide as saucers.

March 22, 2017

What I'm doing is writing every single Facebook friend an actual letter. Why I'm doing it is an attempt to make relationships/friendships that seem almost unreal on Facebook REAL again.

First, I want you to know the high esteem you are and have always been held in in this house. When I first met Willie, he talked so lovingly about Uncle Chuck and Aunt Betty and the Oregon cousins—you were legendary in his childhood. Then I got lucky by getting to go to Oregon and meet you all in person—see where you live, throw hatchets, and eat meat, and be introduced to everyone at the family reunion. To me, that trip is still a top memory, most of all because I got to put faces to names. My expectations were exceeded.

I want you to know that you are loved, appreciated, and remembered (fondly, of course) by Willie, me, and our boys. You are a beloved part of our family—and even though we clearly are not good at keeping in touch, we think about you often.

I received a handwritten letter from Uncle Chuck (aka #547) just over two weeks after I wrote him.

April 10, 2017

Dear Niece Amy and boys,

In the olden days, this is the way we communicated. Three cents and it's on its way. Then that changed—some idiot invented the telephone! That brought on more isolation. Then radio, TV, and the computer—surely the world has come to an end! Oh no! More yet to come—the cell phone! We barely got dial-up on the wall phone—no party line, couldn't listen in on neighbors' conversations, more isolation. So it is good to hear—read!—from you in some medium.

I follow your wacky escapades on FB, even though I don't respond or comment. Haven't much to say. Most of my generation have gone on to greener pastures. I am alone on my brush pile/mountain with my dog. She is older and will be headed out before too long. Still cutting firewood for winter. I am now the oldest in my family. My uncle Arnold recently moved on at ninety-four.

I still throw knives and hatchets/tomahawks, shoot flintlock shotguns and black powder rifles. To think whole generations are growing up not knowing how to do these things. But they all know how to play ball. I digress and am showing my age. Sorry!

Spring is here and the trilliums are blooming, birds are back, and it's peaceful on the mountain. I wonder, out of the 540 letters you have written, how many letter responses have you received? Ha!

Thank you for the kind words, and I truly feel appreciated, deserved or not!

Number 547 was likely the oldest person I wrote a letter to. His paragraph on the evolution of communication, framed in a way that only someone who has lived each stage of adulthood can achieve, speaks to how technology, as much as it offers us almost limitless connections, can make us feel further away from each other.

While anticipating a reply to a text we know someone has read or checking our phones to see who has liked our Facebook or Instagram post might not seem like a lonely act, the wait itself can leave us feeling isolated. It inherently makes us question ourselves. *Why hasn't my friend responded yet? Is anyone going to like my post?*

Additionally, we feel alone because regardless of how many responses we do ultimately receive or how quickly we get them, we remain isolated throughout the entire process of the "conversation."

One-on-one, "old school" communication, on the other hand, leaves no room for such doubts. The other person is right in front of us; we can touch them, see their facial reactions, watch their body movements. They are deliberately here for us, and we for them. We matter. They matter.

Perhaps we've sacrificed reassurance and peace for convenience.

Letter #548

Letter #548 was to a friend in Ohio whom I had met through our sons playing football together. In yet another unsung form of meaningful human interaction, there is nothing, and I mean nothing, like bonding while working the concession stand at a youth sporting event.

Number 548 and I spent several seasons together standing on the sidelines at games and practices, ensuring our younger kids didn't get lost and, yes, trying to get nacho cheese to the desired temperature in a microwave from 1978.

While we discovered that we had a similar sense of humor during the in-person portion of our relationship, it was confirmed and perhaps even amplified in our online link.

March 23, 2017

Okay, so, the way this works is I pull a name randomly out of a box each day and write that person a letter. I've been doing it for a year and a half, and I've written more than 540 people. I've awkwardly written everyone from my high school chemistry teacher to a couple I met at a wedding—once, twenty-five years ago.

And now—finally, today—I pull your name out. What a happy day! Because not only have I seen you in the past twelve months, I know exactly who you are, and I love me some #548!

As much as I loved the time we shared when our boys were playing football, I love being your friend on Facebook, where that same hilarity and family-oriented

*compassion shine through. Really, achieving any sort of
authenticity online is tough, but you manage to do it and
do it so well.*

*So: 1) I'm thankful (sincerely) that our paths crossed
when they originally did—we had little kids, and it was
wild, but you and yours made it not just "better" but
well and truly enjoyable. 2) I'm thankful that we remain
connected via FB. Please know that I'm a fan, so I hope
you keep posting!*

I received a handwritten reply from #548 just shy of three
weeks after I wrote her.

April 15, 2017

Hi Amy!

*I was thrilled to receive your letter. No one writes letters
anymore. Just you and my eighty-two-year-old mother.
She usually slips in $10. You should do that too ☺.
Seriously, it was such a nice surprise. I thought at first
you were asking for money or you were selling something.*

*Yes, I am glad we got to know each other through football.
We really enjoyed our time there. And now we are
"Facebook friends." I love Facebook! It allows me to
maintain friendships without having to actually talk to
anyone! I enjoy your posts very much. You are so funny! I
think we were BFFs in a past life.*

Anyhoo, thank you for brightening my day.

*Wishing your family joy, love, and peace also—or, as my
grandma used to say, "mutual feelings."*

Number 548's comment "I thought at first you were asking for money or you were selling something" speaks volumes about our current culture. While it's understandable, in this age of instantaneous communication, that receiving a handwritten letter would be surprising, what does it say that #548's first takeaway was that I was writing her in hopes of gaining something? How many other recipients had this same reaction? And if I hadn't been writing all the letters and instead had been on the receiving end, what would be my own initial reaction to randomly receiving a handwritten letter have been?

It reminds me of how, early in the Facebook project, I received an out-of-the-blue Facebook message from an old camp friend. I can remember the ding of my phone and then my excitement when I saw who the message was from. My first thought was that she had received one of the letters. When I realized I hadn't written her yet—I was only one hundred letters in and could easily remember who I had and hadn't written—I was even more intrigued. My next thought was *How cool is it she's randomly reaching out to me while I'm doing the same thing with other friends?*

> Hey Amy, so great catching up with you on FB. I have been talking to camp friends lately. It's so fun to chat about camp memories. I have a question for you. Have you heard of Plexus products? I know you have seen my posts.

While I was disappointed that she wasn't just messaging me to say hi or check in, I certainly wasn't surprised or upset that she was selling something. It seemed perfectly natural, because relational marketing is a common element of social media. For the seller, it is a list of potential customers whom they already know and trust, and for the buyer, it's an opportunity to funnel a necessary purchase to a business they want to support, so, in one way, it's a win–win proposition.

On the flip side, the mining of personal contacts for professional gain can leave us assuming everyone wants something from us. That there is no longer any reason for someone to reach out to us randomly without having an ulterior motive.

As much as they have expanded opportunities to foster small businesses, the internet and social media may have cost us the assumption of our friends' goodwill. Fortunately, there is hope—a truth that my exchange with #548 evidences—that we can get past this selling of things and return to the purest form of interpersonal communication. Perhaps it is up to the next generation to make this shift.

Letter #555

The recipient of letter #555 was my only brother, Rick, who is two years younger than I am. We've been close since before I was even forming lucid memories. Even when we were small, we had "serious" talks, discussing the state of our family while perched on one of our beds. Perhaps this happened because we were the two youngest members of our immediate family and no one else really took us seriously. This openness spilled over into our adult lives, where we still talk candidly on a regular basis.

Rick and his wife, Jennifer, were also two of the people I shared the journey of the Facebook project with, so they lived it along with me. His was also one of the handful of letters that made me cry as I wrote it.

March 27, 2017

I've learned SO much from the long process of doing this —it's been truly life-changing. One takeaway that applies to the writing of YOUR letter is that the toughest people to write are the people I'm closest to. I think that's because I want to write a good letter to the people I love. The pressure is much less when I'm writing someone from years ago who may/may not even remember me.

When I look at my life and wonder what's going to happen in the future, I realize that believing in God doesn't mean everything is going to work out the way I want it to. It means that I will be cared for, loved, and supported no matter what happens, and that God will use it all for countless reasons—most of which I'll

*probably never fully understand. It's one of the many
lessons I've learned from Dana and #CONSTANT.*

*Anyway my relationship with you reminds me of how this
works, because when I think of you, I suppose the thing
I'm most thankful for is that in you I've always had and
always will have somebody to weather the storm with. In
short, you make me feel like whatever we face (together or
individually) will be okay because we'll do it together. It's
the GREATEST gift of all.*

*Things with Mom and Dad will get super weird—and,
yes, they'll die. And maybe we'll watch a couple of our
kids struggle, and fight to keep things balanced in our
marriages, but we can still take out the trash in a blue
truck for forty-five minutes and drink two beers each—
because, after all, we're grown-ass adults—and we can
discuss the reality of life as much as we do/don't want to.
Nobody is going to push us to talk about anything real,
but if we do, somebody is going to REALLY care—even if
they don't say it.*

I received a brief text from Rick just seven days after I wrote
him.

April 3, 2017

Thanks for the letter, friend. It means a lot.

His "I'm not saying, but I'm totally saying" reply was perfection, given that we had grown up together in the 1970s, when
our feelings stayed mostly inside our own bodies. There was no
need for him to expand on his message. Even as someone who
struggled with brevity, I got that and respected the hell out of it.

What neither of us could have known in March 2017 was that the date of my letter and my actual words would prove almost prophetic as the future played out. Precisely two years to the day after I had written Rick and forecast that "things will get super weird with Mom and Dad" and they would die, our beloved father passed away suddenly.

Dad was seventy-nine, but he was a robust, almost amazingly healthy guy. He could still run the fifty-yard dash, worked out regularly, did projects that demanded physical strength, and was always on the go. Then, within a matter of days, he was gone.

While I don't have an explanation for the unbelievable timing of my letter to my brother on March 27, 2017, and our father's death on March 27, 2019, I find overwhelming comfort in the fact that I said what I said when I said it.

It was hard, and our hearts were broken, but we did it, as my letter indicated, together. And we didn't have to say anything, because it had already been said. We looked at each other across the bed that Dad died in, and we already knew that being there together was everything. We weren't alone.

There is no way we can predict the future, but boldly making the effort to say what is on our hearts will always turn out to be a good thing.

Letter #556

⤫

Letter #556 was to a guy I had met at a party in England. It was my dear friend Yvonne's fiftieth birthday, and I had returned to the UK with the help of my much older sister, who as a flight attendant had standby privileges that she was generously willing to share.

Number 556 was friends with Yvonne's son, Matthew, whom I have known since he was ten. Though I had heard plenty about #556, I don't know that I had ever met him before our paths crossed at the birthday celebration. Where I was pushing fifty, he wasn't even twenty-five. Where I drove a minivan, had a C-section scar, and lived near a cornfield, he drove a MINI, sounded like James Bond, and met his mates at a pub for a pint.

As the night of the party wore on, I ended up drinking a series of adult beverages with #556 and discussing first sports statistics and then our deepest feelings. Our shared love of competition turned into a meaningful discussion about our very existence.

Then we became Facebook official.

Then I wrote him a letter.

March 31, 2017

You and I are very uniquely connected. Not only did we have an epic discussion about sports stats at Yvonne's fiftieth birthday party, but we are closely linked to the same family. Basically, we have BFFs who are in the same family—you have Matthew (whom my son is named after) and I have Yvonne. So we are extensions of the same unit, and therefore we care deeply about the same set of people. And not only are we statistical badasses, we are our people's people! #yes!

I sincerely hope that wherever and however this finds you, you truly are happy and well. I also hope that whatever lies ahead is good and fun and full of love. #cheesybuttrue

The truth is, you and I are destined to attend a few weddings in the future, so here's to having a couple of adult beverages and celebrating life together with our mutual people! #cantwait

All the best to you and your family,

Amy W. D.

Your friend in REAL life

I never received a reply from #556 and have no idea if he even got the letter. Given that it was one of the more awkward ones I penned, I'm totally okay with that and am satisfied with just hoping it was received in the spirit in which I sent it.

While it served as a warning that buzzed friending has consequences, letter #556 also attested to the viability of relationships based on connections between people's people. It's how love works. We love someone or a group of someones, and, naturally, they are also loved by others. We may not know these "others" intimately, but we are linked by the love we share for the same people. We have the same "taste" in friends, and we likely have similar core values.

We all have a relationship graph, with circles representing our people and then lines connecting them with us and others. Only by viewing the chart from above can we begin to see how many amazing links exist—how we are bound, in meaningful ways, to so many people.

The lines between us, regardless of how far they extend from the center, all represent love. We are loved, and have opportunities to love, in more ways than we can ever imagine.

Letter #564

The recipient of letter #564 was a friend from camp. We had been counselors together for just one summer, 1989, but had managed, as with so many other relationships from Olympia, to make a significant connection. She is smart, outgoing, funny, and ambitious. I knew from word of mouth, and social media, that she had started her own public relations firm sometime between graduating from college and the early 2000s.

We became Facebook friends in 2008, and sometime after that she sent me a request to follow her firm's Facebook page, which I accepted. This led to my seeing a post on her professional page that resonated with me in a big way.

April 10, 2017

Not only do I remember you very fondly from our shared time at Camp Olympia, and not only do I love following snapshots of your life and that of your beautiful people, via FB, but we have a more recent personal and meaningful connection. Ironically, it's something you know nothing about, which is why am so excited about this letter ☺!

Okay, here's the deal. Some time ago—years, likely—your firm's page posted an image explaining "the creative process" and offered the following steps: 1) This is awesome. 2) This is tricky. 3) This is crap. 4) I am crap. 5) This might be okay. 6) This is awesome. Anyway, I read it just as I was trying to get myself remotivated on a book idea I had, and not only did it inspire me, I took a screen shot of it, have kept it through a couple of phones, and have looked at it over and over as I experienced, fully, each of the steps. I so connected with it that—and this is the best part—I FINISHED THE BOOK (all 378 pages of it) last week, and then, amazingly, I drew your name to write a letter for my FB experiment two days later.

WHAT?

That's crazy good and 100 percent one of the best stories to come out of this so far.

So please know that you have inspired me, despite all the years and miles that separate us, and that you (yes, via FB, but first via real-life friendship) are one of the top ten reasons I finished writing an actual book. It makes me think about how we can go through life wondering if anything we do makes a difference only to find out, every once in a while, quite randomly and perhaps in horrible handwriting, that we are rocking people's worlds.

About two months after I wrote her, I received a handwritten reply from #564. It was a colorful note with "Thank you" printed on the front. Under this, she hand-wrote "for reaching out to me!"

June 16, 2017

I was so excited to receive your letter! It was so good to hear about what is going on in your world! I think it is an awesome fact that my post inspired you to the point of finishing your book. I had no idea that any of my posts would be that impactful for anyone!

I would love to hear more about your FB experiment as

well. It is a nice way to keep up with people, but I often wonder how it is affecting my children. All they see is everyone having these happy, perfect lives, and I wonder how it affects their self-esteem and self-image.

Perhaps it's true that social media posts have no real way of changing people's minds, especially if they are framed with negativity or, even worse, hate. That said, what if sharing a nugget of wisdom or truth that resonated with us enables us to magically reach out to someone and help them without our even knowing it? What if the good we are trying to spread is really blossoming out there in the great unknown?

In researching this book, I went back and looked at #564's post about the creative process. It was dated April 15, 2014, and received a whopping total of six "likes" (a number that included me) and three comments (which did not include anything from me). The responses were "LOL," "This happens to me pretty much every day!" and "Love!"

Combined, these reactions can hardly be labeled "strong," much less "trending" or "viral." But, unbeknownst to #564, her post not only stayed with me but changed my whole creative path.

Gauging "success" on social media entails keeping a count of who feels strongly enough about a post to go on record with a reaction. When applied before we share, this metric has the power to make us second-guess ourselves and, perhaps, to prevent us from posting something that may be of real value to others. Who wants to share something that gets only three likes? But maybe "likes" and comments are the *least* effective way of measuring real impact.

Letter #579

Letter #579 was to a friend I met in high school. She was a year older than I was, and though we knew of each other, we weren't ever close or in the same friend group. Where I was a funny, nonmusical musician who made decent grades and lacked self-confidence, #579 was a vocal leader, an accomplished performer, and an honor roll student.

I can remember "friending" #579 and almost being amazed that she accepted my request. It was almost like I was finally in the "in" crowd, receiving some sort of validation that I had always wanted.

While I certainly admired #579 in high school, I didn't ever get the sense that she looked down on me. I just always assumed she didn't even really know who I was.

What I did "know," or what I gleaned from social media, was that, like so many of my Facebook friends, she didn't share my political coordinates. Where she was more left, I was more right. But as I wrote the letters—a span that included the 2016 presidential election—my position on the political spectrum was becoming more fluid.

April 19, 2017

I appreciate—very much—being your friend on FB and being reconnected. I'm especially glad of the timing and that we rode out the last election cycle together. Though I didn't agree with every one of your posts or views, I do respect—so very much—your passion and insight. In fact, I feel like I learned so much from you throughout last year. I am now a woman without a "side" politically—

much of that because I don't want to be affiliated with hate and fear. I want you to know that your posts helped me to see things differently. I think you are incredibly brave (especially given the tight box we all grew up in), and I love how you are willing—always—to take a firm stand on either side of an issue, regardless of where "your side" stands on it.

I hope you know that you are making a difference, despite how many "likes" your post gets or who says what. I'm glad we're friends and I'm glad we're different—it's what makes the world better, and it's how change really begins.

Of all the people I didn't expect to hear back from in writing, #579 would have been in the top ten. That made pulling her response out of my mailbox an actual rush. This was what "Wow!" felt like.

Also of note is the fact that I felt this sense of awe despite the fact that I was at the end of my project. Human interaction, as it turns out, is so unpredictable and potentially jam-packed with goodness, that even the most seasoned participant can still experience an unexpected jolt of sheer joy.

June 9, 2017

Hey Amy,

Sorry it has taken me a while to write back. I really want to thank you for your words to me about Facebook. While I can see both sides of it—good and bad—I do think it has the potential to help us see each other more fully and to hear and consider the views and experiences of people we know but maybe don't really know or understand.

I am filled with hope and optimism when I hear from people like you. I'm also really taken by your effort to get back to pen/paper, especially when I realized I don't even have any stationery anymore!

Take care of yourself. Thank you. Stay in touch.

Sometimes it seems like we live in a world where we are expected to agree with every individual with whom we surround ourselves. As if "our people," in order to truly be our people, must be on the same page about politics, societal issues, and even our specific brand of religion and/or spirituality. Can we even consider someone a "friend" if their compass doesn't point the same way as ours?

What if instead we consider that we might be better served by including in our lives people who aren't like us in every way? What if we welcomed people who we assumed wouldn't welcome us? What if we opened our hearts and listened without prejudice? What if we didn't put any limitations or qualifications on who we could consider our friends?

Love is inclusive. It simply cannot leave people out. That's impossible!

Letter #580

Letter #580 was officially the final letter of the Facebook project. I had written two letters the day before, a Wednesday, and decided to leave the last letter until the next morning.

When I woke up that day, my very first thought was, *Today is the last day I'll ever write a Facebook letter.* As much as I felt pride and excitement, the biggest emotional component of that moment was relief. I don't think I really understood the burden the letters were to me personally until I finished writing them. Perhaps the undeniable driving force that had pushed me to finish no matter what had pushed me right to the edge. Physically, I could feel it in my hands; the callus on the ring finger of my right hand had grown even more and now bled regularly. I felt as if I were a balloon, but instead of the air being let out of me, it was all my feelings. I was, emotionally speaking, flying unpredictably through the room, making a loud hissing sound as I went. When all my feelings had finally been sucked out, I lay crumpled up behind the couch alongside a grape that had morphed into a raisin.

That said, I also felt waves of adrenaline and excitement. It was a lot like the first 5k I ran in Memphis—I was hurt, I was struggling, but I was just about to freaking do it.

The final Facebook letter was to the girl who grew up across the street from me. She was a year younger, but we were neighbors from the time I went to second grade through my senior year of high school.

We had not kept in touch, of course, outside the confines of Facebook.

April 20, 2017

Dear #580,

Greetings! I hope this finds you and your family all happy and well. So, we'll get started with the obvious question: Why am I writing you an actual, "old school" letter? Well, other than clearly losing my mind, recently I have begun wondering what it means to be "friends" on Facebook. It all started rather innocently in 2015, when I wanted to send a Facebook friend a condolence card, as her fifteen-year-old son, Parker, had died of cancer. It was a great plan—that is, until I realized that not only did I not have her address, I wasn't even sure where she lived. It was a turning point for me. Could I really be friends with five hundred–plus people without being required to personally invest in most of the relationships? And, though I enjoyed social media, had it compromised my definition of words like "friendship"? That's when I first wondered what would happen if I tried to write ALL of my FB people a letter. Would it allow me to make deposits in my relationship accounts?

Well, after 570-plus of these letters, I can tell you that not only have I become considerably more invested in people, but along the way the project has managed to alter the course of my life. What's changed the most is my own heart. Who knew that each of these blips on my news feed were actual individuals with AMAZING stories and all living a version of REAL life? And who knew that being connected to each was far more than an exercise in randomness and instead a very deliberate pattern that meant God had been looking out for me through relationships from the very beginning? As it turned out, I was luckier than I ever could have imagined.

Your letter and you specifically are super special on several levels. First, you are one of the very few people whom I've known so long that I don't remember when we met. I'm assuming it was when we moved into our house on Creekview in 1976. Were you there then? You are one of the very few people I knew throughout growing up and whose parents I can still picture to this day—washing their cars, working in the yard. We are from the same "hood." We started out in life literally just steps away from each other. It's a common bond that must mean we have similarities that we're not even aware of.

It makes me thankful for FB that we can stay somewhat connected. Without it, I'd never have seen your beautiful children and your husband, or have been able to get a sense of what your adult life is like. It truly is an honor! It's funny, when I see pictures of your son specifically, it takes me all the way back to the intersection of Morningcrest and Creekview. That's amazing!

And now I have questions—like, how are your mom and dad? Your brothers? Do you keep in touch with anyone else? How are YOU?

My parents—Dick and Sue—live in Elkins Lake in Huntsville. Kim lives in the Woodlands and works for United. Rick lives at our family place in New Waverly with his wife and FIVE kids (#yikes)—he flips properties and owns rental units in Huntsville.

We've been in Ohio since 2007. I met my husband, Willie, at Camp Olympia in 1991. We married in 1993 and had our first son, Will, in 1997. We moved to England from

2002 to 2005 and had Matthew in 2006 in Houston. I graduated from Texas Tech in 1991 and am a freelance writer. Despite the winters, we like it here and have made a life of it. Still, we plan to return home to Texas once Willie retires.

The other thing that makes this letter—your letter—so significant is that it is the final letter of this long project. It's taken 1.5 years and almost six hundred stamps, but here we are. Honestly, I didn't think I'd actually finish, so what went from being a ridiculous idea has been transformed into something I'll write a book about.

The way it's worked is, I've pulled a name out of a box each day, randomly, and written that person a letter. It makes the fact that your name waited all the way to the end amazing. I think it's fitting that it's you—someone I've known my entire life and whom I'm tied to so significantly.

If I've learned anything from all of this, it's that each of us—no matter how shiny and wonderful things may seem on the surface—is living a REAL life. That means that while, yes, we are blessed, we also inevitably encounter the challenges and difficulties that come with life and make us stumble. I sincerely hope that your version of real life is more joy-filled than hard.

Until we meet again, thanks for being my friend for forty-plus years. That's not something you can say to everyone.

I wish you and yours joy, love, and most of all peace!

Love, Amy W. D.

Your friend in REAL life

It was a wrap. I put my pen down and sighed heavily. Then I got up and literally danced around my office, pumping my fists and flailing. When the physical celebration ended, I sat back down at my computer, opened that week's college football article, and began to write. It wasn't that I wasn't acknowledging the moment for all of its blazing glory, for its impossibility; I was simply using my normal routine as a shield to protect me from an attack of my own feelings.

It was coming at me from all sides. I felt proud enough to get the proverbial "big head," to buy into my own personal exceptionalism, yet I knew it wasn't about me, that instead the project was all due to something so much bigger than I was that I couldn't even use my precious words to describe it.

Then there was the love. So much love had been exchanged in those letters that I was stuffed full in a good way. I didn't need to throw up; I needed to dance with ribbon sticks. And sing Disney princess songs. And sprinkle glitter around my house and twirl while somebody blew bubbles in my direction. It was like a nuclear reaction going off inside my own heart. And I had no idea what I was supposed to do with it.

Later, when Matthew got off the bus from school, I decided we would make a big deal of mailing the final letter. He, along with Willie and Will, had walked every step of the project with me, so it seemed fitting. I wasn't sure I'd post about it, but I wanted to record the moment for, if nothing else, posterity.

Ironically, we didn't go to the post office nearest our house, where I had mailed the bulk of the letters from, because its only drop-off options were inside—a public spot that people used regularly—and the drive-through. Since I wanted a photo, I needed to go to a site that wasn't busy and that I could get to on foot. The good news was that between Dana's letters and the Facebook project, I knew the location of literally every blue post office box within twenty miles of our house.

So we went to a box I'd used only a couple of times, located in a bank parking lot in front of a grocery store we didn't frequent. It took about seventeen tries, and Matthew was highly annoyed, but we finally got a good shot of us inserting the final letter into the blue box.

When I got home, I texted Dana the picture of Matthew and me, along with an additional photo of the empty box that, just a year and a half earlier, had contained the names of all my Facebook friends.

> The Box is empty! I wrote and mailed the final letter today. God's love for you and your family delivered in 580 envelopes. #truestory #dropthemic #youcantmakethisstuffup #loveyou #CONSTANT!

Next, I decided to post the photo at the postbox on social media. It was the only way to let all 580 of the letter recipients know that I had indeed reached the finish line.

> Matthew and I mailing the final Facebook letter! What started as a ridiculous idea one year and eight months ago became, letter by letter, a life-changing experience. #reallifefriends #mindblown #heartchanged #godsriveraloveisLEGIT #peaceoutfacebook #thanksfriends #myhandhurts

Though I received a reply from #580 via Facebook messenger on May 12, about thirty days later, I also got a handwritten letter. It was an epic, eight-page update on her life.

June 16, 2017

It was wonderful getting your letter and hearing all about you and your family and your amazing adventure to reach out to your Facebook friends in such a personal way! I love it!

I now know how my parents felt. There's this huge difference between generations, and for so long I never understood how my parents felt! It's all falling into place, and I clearly see the generation gap! I think it's an aha moment. . . . I'm trying to be open to the differences and open to doing things more than just one way, but, man, with all the electronics and social media today, I feel like I'm being left in the dust!

Though the Facebook project is complete, I can still feel it reverberating to this day and recognize it in every layer of not only who I am but who I'll continue to become. I fully anticipate this to be the case for the rest of my life.

In the words of Matthew when we mailed letter #580, "Mom, this is the biggest achievement of your entire life." He was only eleven years old at that moment, but he nailed it.

June 2020

*O*n the spring of 2020, Dana and I began speaking on the phone on a regular basis. Though that mode of communication had become more and more a part of our relationship, we didn't talk daily until the COVID pandemic shut the world down that March.

Dana was isolated at home and not teaching. While I had worked from home since I began my freelance writing career, that spring the rest of my family joined me, setting up remote spaces for employment and school.

As the lockdown began, with no serious forethought, Dana and I began to talk while we walked every day. It allowed us both to get out of the house, exercise, and survive the uncertainty by discussing both the crisis and the minute details of our daily lives endlessly.

One day, Dana shared a series of profound thoughts she had had. "I started thinking about the end of my time at camp in 1986," she said, "and how I must have gone around and said goodbye to everyone before I left."

"I've never even thought of that," I replied.

"Since you were staying on when I left," she continued, "there must have been a moment when I said goodbye to you, but I don't remember it."

"Neither do I," I said.

"I started thinking about how God must have been laughing hysterically as we hugged and said goodbye," she said. "We were thinking, *Well, have a nice life, 'cause I probably won't ever see you again*, while God was chuckling, and knowing, 'If you only knew what I have planned for you two.'"

When I hung up the phone that day, I couldn't stop thinking about what Dana had said. Seriously, who would ever have thought, back in 1986, that the brief, seemingly meaningless encounter between us would explode into something so profound that we'd never fully understand it? That after thirty years of silence and doing life apart, we'd be connected in a way that not only changed our own lives but had the power to transform the hearts of people we didn't even know? Although, because of Parker, I'll never frame this as a "good" thing, its impact and the positive layers associated with it are undeniable.

The dichotomous nature of our entire connection is encapsulated in a thought that Dana has shared with me repeatedly. "I will always wish that you were just a distant memory, somebody I don't even know," she says, "because that would mean Parker was still here."

I still write Dana once a week, every Sunday, and she writes me back one or two times a month. We also text each other on a regular basis. When she's teaching, she often calls me on the way to school. As of 2020, seldom does a day go by without some sort of contact between the two of us.

We also see each other. My family and I visit the Riveras' home, and they stay at our house. Our move from Ohio to Houston in June 2019 makes these trips much more feasible.

It's also given us the opportunity to physically show up for each other. I've been to Dana's daughters' weddings and baby showers, and she was at my dad's memorial service. When we moved back to Texas, Matthew and I were the last ones to arrive, making the seventeen-hour trek only to wearily get out of the car and find box after box stacked in room after room of our new house. Just as I felt fully overwhelmed, who came around the corner, out of nowhere, with a bottle of champagne in hand, but Dana and Jim Rivera? They spent the next three days helping us unpack and set up our house. By the time they left, it was a home.

What's also developed over time is our shared sense of humor and love of hilarity. I don't know that I've ever laughed more with another human being than I have with Dana. I also don't know anyone whom I could text at nine o'clock on a Monday night and say, "I found pilgrim costumes; let's wear them to Thanksgiving" and get "I'm all in; I'll take a medium" as a reply.

I'm also in close contact with each of Jim and Dana's four daughters—Alli, Lauren, Madelyn, and Peyton—and communicate with their sons-in-law and many of their close friends.

While a lot of the discourse between Dana and me and Dana's girls and me is about day-to-day life and shenanigans, the majority of our exchanges, especially via text, continue to involve #CONSTANT prayer.

I suppose I've known this for a long time, but the Riveras are my people and I know, in a part of me where no questions exist, that I am supposed to—as if it were my actual reason for being born—look out for them, and love the crap out of them, and cover them in prayer. Constantly. As is the case with so much of this story, it's not deliberate, as in "here's what I'm going to do"; instead, it's that my heart knows exactly what to do.

I've often wondered what I'm supposed to call Dana—how

she, from a category standpoint, fits into my relationship chart. Is she my pen pal, my friend, my divine connection, my what?

The thought initially presented itself when I was composing a post on Facebook, sharing a few photos from one of Dana's and my in-person meetings. While I'm not sure what label I used for her in that specific post, I did think to ask her the next time I saw her.

"What should I even call you?" I asked.

"You call me your bestie!" she replied.

Epilogue

While there is no way to list all of the life-changing observations I made both during and after the Facebook project, I have continued—from the day after I wrote the final letter until the present—to record thoughts in my original journal. It's a way to keep the memory, and the impact, of the following lessons fresh and to add new insights as they come to me. It's a reminder to never stop growing. To never assume that our hearts can't be transformed. To never, ever think we're done learning. As of this book's publication, these are the most important takeaways from the Facebook project:

1. Noninstantaneous communication—in combination with love—is a game changer. Not knowing when someone receives or reads a message you send is freeing. The opportunity to think about what you're saying before you send it, and the time to consider others' words/thoughts without the pressure to respond results in a more open, deeply thought-out form of communication. It totally changes the way you think.

2. Social media relationships lack realness because they don't require us to invest, or to be particularly deliberate, to sustain them. While Facebook connects us, it can also leave us feeling isolated and can cause us to question our friends' motives. For all its legitimate advantages, technology has redefined the terms "friendship" and "relationship."

3. Behind every profile, post, and picture are real, imperfect people living real, imperfect lives. We can't comprehend the realness of other people's lives any more than they can understand the realness of our own situations.

4. Our value, on- or offline, has nothing to do with the amount of "likes" or comments and/or validation we receive.

5. Boldly reaching out to someone and expressing ourselves is always a good thing. As much as our loving words might mean to those we direct them to, saying them deliberately will also change our own hearts forever.

6. You don't need a response from someone to make a difference in their life. Though we will get glimpses, we can never know the full impact that our actions have on other people. While we can't gauge the ripple effect of our attempts at goodness, we should never stop trying.

7. There is something going on in our worlds that is bigger than those things we can feel, touch, and see, and that are irrefutable facts. Being unsure, and mystified, and confident in things that can't be proven are exceptionally good ways to be.

8. My life will *never* be the same. I'm the one most changed by all of this. I'm more grateful and empathetic and refuse to accept that anything can separate people. I've also experienced a deepening in many of my relationships. People receive and treat me differently because of the letters. This clearly happens because of love and the power not of my own words but of being treated like an individual in a world depersonalized by social media.

9. I wish I could get into a big room with all 580 of the people I wrote a letter to. I would love to hug each and every recipient. If that actually happened, I think 1) my heart would explode and I'd laugh so hard I'd nearly die, and 2) I'd spend days afterward feeling guilty that I hadn't really talked to each person.

10. Love is the most powerful force on the planet. It transcends politics, beliefs, circumstances, and any other factor that sepa-

rates one individual from another. Hate simply cannot win in a climate of individual love. You can't be a hater after you reach out to people individually, especially when they respond in kind. Not one single thing can separate people who strive to love each other unconditionally.

11. You never know when a seed is being planted. It's a mystery that can be solved only by looking backward. My story is rock-solid proof that a series of life-changing events can line up magically without the people involved even knowing it. For me, this is how God works.

12. My extraordinary journey didn't start when Parker Rivera lost his battle with cancer, but it is the event on which the story of my own life pivoted dramatically. This means that my beloved friend Dana's greatest tragedy ultimately altered the course of my own journey and that of so many others. I will *never* be at one with that. It will never make sense to me or seem right. Her unthinkable personal loss and the cost to her heart will, for the rest of my life, be impossible to comprehend.

The story I have told in this book is simply my personal experience. It's not a guide for or recommendation on how to do anything. Instead, it's an example of what love can do. I've come to believe that each of us has our own unique path. Rather than urging one another to take the exact same road that we're on, perhaps the real way forward is supporting, loving, and encouraging one another, regardless of our different paths.

Acknowledgments

First and foremost, a sincere thank-you to the 580 real-life friends to whom I wrote Facebook letters. Thank you for responding and not responding. For sharing your story, your insight, and your wisdom. For giving me your mailing addresses and for filling my mailbox, inbox, and heart with so much love. While it was impossible to include all our individual communications here, I believe the spirit of each and every word is well represented. An additional thank-you to all those who signed on, anonymously, to have their specific stories included in this book—your blind support is priceless.

To Annie Tucker, the most important person in the telling of this story: From our very first meeting, and even after reading my one-million-word first draft, you had a clear vision of how I could best format and present *Dear Dana*. Then you patiently walked through every single word with me, pushing me to get it right, demanding the hard work and deep consideration that the story deserved. I hope you're as proud of the results of our teamwork as I am. There will never be good enough words to thank you. #showdonttell #dreamteam #hereforit

To Brooke Warner: You and your team (I'm talking about you, Samantha Strom) were the only ones who gave *You Cannot Mess This Up* any serious consideration, and then you doubled down by enthusiastically supporting *Dear Dana*. Thank you for your commitment to fighting for stories like mine.

To Sherry Dillon Maze, my second-grade teacher: Thank you for teaching me to read and write. Without you, there would be no books by me.

To Corby and Barbara Robertson and Chris and Pam

Gilbert: Thank you for founding Camp Olympia, the font of life-changing relationships.

To Tommy and Kathy Ferguson, the longtime directors of Camp Olympia: Thank you for creating the culture where this story began and flourished.

To my Camp Olympia family: Thank you for being my people for forty years.

To Tara Beck Bissonnet, aka Kat: Thank you for enthusiastically supporting me as this story unfolded and then being a champion of this book before it was even a thing. Your innate wisdom has been invaluable in keeping things in perspective.

To Sue, Lee, and Emma Shibley: Thank you for bravely sharing your grief experience. In my humble opinion, this story is one of the reasons God made us across-the-street neighbors on Black Birch Drive. LFATS.

To the people of Christ Church UMC, Kettering, Ohio: The moment I first became inspired to write Dana and Parker, I was surrounded not only by the walls of a building we shared but by each of you. Thanks for praying alongside me and for creating an environment where God could get all up in my business.

To Team #CONSTANT: Kristi and Ron Lamb, Scott and Mary Barr, Sarah and Chad Vier, Carolyn and Dave Bates, Dawn and Andrew Koenig, Shonda and Trey Hiers, Rye and Chris Walsh, the Christ UMC Men of Integrity, Sue Shibley, Caroline Hamm, Christy Jung McAlister, Stephanie Weaver, Elizabeth Sarradet, Rebecca Mouk, Susan and Kelly Hall, Monica Wells, Kimber Weinland, Amy and Craig Moss, Matthew Daughters, Clay and Deanna Barr, Estelle Bee Weinland, Fiona Grace Weinland, Clara Sue Weinland, Otto Oscar Weinland, Finn Eugene Weinland, Christel Kirkpatrick, Deena and Aaron Weast, Becky Clinton, Leigh Bowman, Hannah Muller Cortes, Lauren Christner, Becky Muller, Debbie Stubblefield, Lisa Youngblood

Wright, Tommy and Kathy Ferguson, Will Daughters, Virginia Lyons, Caden Barr, Rachel Dale, Mike Roberts, Connie Collmorgen, June Cowan, Arlene Gates, Rick and Jen Weinland, Emily Lawrence, Kathy and Bobby Davis, Grace Barr, Sonna Young, Willie Daughters, Lydia Mathis, Joanna Gaines, Kayla Allen, Diane Taaffe, Julie and Robert Burnett, Lory Mulder, Sheri Robinson, Carrie Mathis, Missy Buchanan, Patty Lanning, Floyd and Shelly Daughters, Hogan Daughters, Morgan Daughters, Jagan Daughters, Jane Wood, Annie Tucker, Dick and Sue Weinland, and countless others: Thank you for your continued commitment to cover the Rivera family in love and prayer. Keep praying!

To Julia Turner: As was the case with my first book, I hope you see your indelible impact throughout these pages. Our deep conversations not only are reflected here but are a part of the better me that I have become by being your friend.

To Mary Barr: This story would not be this story without you and me being BFFs in Dayton, Ohio. Thanks for being the most enthusiastic emotional designated driver in the history of friendships.

To Sue Weinland: One of my favorite things about the process of rewriting this book is how you and I discussed every facet of it as it happened. So not only is there a lot of your influence as a mom in the actual story, there's also a lot of your impact as a friend in how I ultimately told it. I love you, and, contrary to popular belief, you don't own me.

To Dick Weinland, my beloved father, whom we lost in 2019: You called the Facebook project "a great social experiment." I'm so grateful you knew about the letters and met both Jim and Dana. Thank you for a lifetime of examples of how to live outside all the boxes and then the freedom to choose my own path. Your fingerprints are all over this story.

To Willie, Will, and Matthew Daughters: I can't believe how many times each of you has blindly supported me. "Hey! I'm going to write a book, so everyone shut up." "Okay, Mom, it's going to be a best seller." "Hey! I want to write personal letters to your school friends and work associates." "That's great, Mom; here are the addresses." How I didn't screw up and get hooked up with the wrong people is beyond me—but God knew. Thank you for believing in me when there was literally nothing to believe in. Any success is shared, and don't think, even for a fleeting second, that I don't know that I couldn't have done any of this without each of you. I can't wait until family game night, and I look forward to going to bed mad at everybody.

To all of Dana and Jim's family and close friends, especially Angela and Jason Vesper (the Gappers); Cheryl Guillory (#okcheryl); Hailey Granger; Renee (Station 6), Dustin, Lauren, Riley, Lilly, and Finley Marchand; Heidi and Durk Viator; Dave and Charlene Hamilton; Madonna and Buddy Brasseaux; Lynn and Ina Dugas; Laurie and Jay Bivins; Tom, Cindy, Katie, and Chase Bouchie; Kim and John Bourgeois; Aunt Jo Villar Stafford; Gwen and Phil Bertrand; Erin and Art Walsh; Ken and Jennifer Jackson; Paula Broussard; Andria Thibodeaux; Vickie Dunn; Chris Cormier; Kate Decker; Gabi Bivins; Kacky Bertrand; Claire Vesper; Anne-Claire "feelings" Viator; and the Running Hens: Thank you for welcoming my family and me with literally open arms and for letting me crash your showers, parties, homes, and lives.

To Jacque Romero, William Hadden, Collin Murphy, and T-Dog Davis, the boys' club that is more like a brotherhood than a brother-in-law-hood: Thank you for being our people and for taking such good care of the people we love.

To Alli Romero, Lauren Hadden, Madelyn Murphy, and Peyton Davis: Thank you for accepting my intrusion into your lives, each in your own special and unique way. Your love and grace have a lot to do with this story even happening. As for each of your friendships, they are individually and collectively among the greatest, yet totally unexpected, gifts of my life. #CONSTANT

To Jim Rivera, the super-nice guy I met at camp in 1985: It was our two paths that God first caused to intersect in what I believe was a very deliberate way. Thank you not only for welcoming me into your home but for generously receiving me into your life and your family's. I am sorry about being loud and disruptive and for not being better at cornhole. And I thank you for all the sandwiches you have ever made me/will make me in the future. This story doesn't happen without you being who you are.

To Dana Dugas Rivera: Though I'll never, ever be "right" with how "us" came about, your friendship is beyond anything I could ever have imagined. Somehow, some way, you have become the "friend I always needed." I know that I know that I *know* that you have done more for me, and y'all have done more for us, than I/we have ever done for you/yours. God decided.

To Parker Rivera: Though I've not yet met you, I feel a connection to you that makes no sense. For all that I don't know, I am rock-solid convinced that *your ongoing relationship* with Jesus is why this story unfolded as it did. I look forward to the biggest hug, and an eternity of shenanigans, on the other side of the thin veil that separates here from there.

To God: While I'll never, at least on this side of heaven, be able to comprehend the complexities of your hand in this story, I do know that for me personally it was the vehicle by which our relationship—yours and mine—was transformed from close acquaintances to BFFs. As it turns out, not only are you my Lord and Savior, you are my best friend. I absolutely cannot wait to see what you do next. *This is all—all 1,000,000 percent—you.* Thank you.

About the Author

A native Houstonian and a graduate of the Texas Tech University, Amy W. Daughters has been a freelance writer for more than a decade—covering college football and sometimes talking about her feelings. Her debut novel, *You Cannot Mess This Up: A True Story That Never Happened* (She Writes Press, 2019), was selected as the Silver Winner for Humor in the 2019 *Foreword* INDIES and the Overall Winner for Humor/Comedy in the 2020 Next Generation Indie Awards. An amateur historian, hack golfer, charlatan fashion model, and regular on the ribbon dancing circuit, Amy—a proud former resident of Blackwell, England, and Dayton, Ohio—currently lives in Tomball, Texas, a suburb of Houston. She is married to a foxy computer person, Willie (53), and is the lucky mother of two amazing sons, Will (23) and Matthew (15).

SELECTED TITLES FROM SHE WRITES PRESS

She Writes Press is an independent publishing company
founded to serve women writers everywhere.
Visit us at www.shewritespress.com.

Never Sit If You Can Dance: Lessons from My Mother by Jo Giese. $16.95,
978-1-63152-533-9. Babe was no goodie two-shoes: she drank, danced,
and stayed up very late. She favored colorful clothes, liked giving parties, adored her husband, and always told her daughter, "Never sit if
you can dance." Told with lighthearted good humor, this a charming
tale of the way things used to be—and probably still should be.

Motherlines: Letters of Love, Longing, and Liberation by Patricia Reis.
$16.95, 978-1-63152-121-8. In her midlife search for meaning, and
longing for maternal connection, Patricia Reis encounters uncommon
women who inspire her journey and discovers an unlikely confidante
in her aunt, a free-spirited Franciscan nun.

Renewable: One Woman's Search for Simplicity, Faithfulness, and Hope by
Eileen Flanagan. $16.95, 978-1-63152-968-9. At age forty-nine, Eileen
Flanagan had an aching feeling that she wasn't living up to her youth-
ful ideals or potential, so she started trying to change the world—and
in doing so, she found the courage to change her life.

*The Clarity Effect: How Being More Present Can Transform Your Work
and Life* by Sarah Harvey Yao. $16.95, 978-1-63152-958-0. A practical,
strategy-filled guide for stressed professionals looking for clarity,
strength, and joy in their work and home lives.

Brave(ish): A Memoir of a Recovering Perfectionist by Margaret Davis
Ghielmetti. $16.95, 978-1-63152-747-0. An intrepid traveler sets off at
forty to live the expatriate dream overseas—only to discover that she
has no idea how to live even her own life. Part travelogue and part
transformation tale, Ghielmetti's memoir, narrated with humor and
warmth, proves that it's never too late to reconnect with our authentic
selves—if we dare to put our own lives first at last.